Approach To Neuropsychology

Dr. Juan Moisés de la Serna

www.juanmoisesdelaserna.es/en

Translated by Susana Hyder

Preface

When we speak of neuropsychology we are talking about one of the branches that has experienced the most growth in the past few years since it makes use of the advances of both psychology and neuroscience.

The field of neuropsychology embraces theoretical aspects as well as those in practice regarding disorders and traumas.

This is a field that is ever more in demand due to the great benefits that it offers to patients.

Table of Contents

Dedicated to my parents

Acknowledgements

I would like to take this opportunity to thank all the people who collaborated with their contributions towards the completion of this book. Especially Dr. David Lavilla Muñoz, Tenured Professor of Digital Communication and New Trends at the European University. Also Dr. Daniela Galindo Bermúdez, President of Hablando con Julis [Talking with Julis]: The solution to communication and learning for people with disabilities.

Legal Notice

This book may not be reproduced in its entirety or in part, uploaded to any information storage and retrieval system, or transmitted in any form by any means whether electronic, or mechanical, including photocopying, by recording or any other means without prior written permission from the author and copyright owner. Infringement of the aforementioned rights may constitute a criminal offense under intellectual property legislation. (Art. 270 ff of the Penal Code).

Refer to C.E.D.R.O.(Centro Español de Derechos Reprográficos) if you need to photocopy or scan any portion of this work. You may contact C.E.D.R.O. online at www.conlicencia.com or by phone at 91 702 19 70 / 93 272 04 47.

© Juan Moisés de la Serna, 2018

"Approach to Neuropsychology"

Written By Juan Moises de la Serna

Copyright © 2018 Juan Moises de la Serna

Distributed by TeakTime.

https://www.traduzionelibri.it

Translated by Susana Hyder

Chapter 1 Neural Foundations of the Brain

Neuropsychology arises from the union of two branches of study, psychology and medicine, their subject of study being psychological processes, memory, attention, and language, how these develop with age and whether they are altered by developmental disorders and problems associated with traumas, illness or old age.

Regarding the brain, it is important to understand its neural foundations, especially in regards to the psychological capabilities that neuropsychology deals with.

Anatomically, the cerebral cortex is divided by the central sulcus, which leaves the right hemisphere to one side and the left to the other side. Below both of these is found the diencephalon which are interior structures (the thalamus, subthalamus, hypothalamus, epithalamus, metathalamus and third ventricle) which connects to the brain stem (midbrain, pons, and the medulla oblongata).

On the other hand, the hemispheres may be divided in, frontal lobe (located in the front part of the brain), parietal lobe (behind the frontal lobe, above the temporal lobe and in front of the occipital lobe), temporal lobe (beneath the middle part of the cortex, right behind the temples), and the occipital lobe (situated in the front part of the brain).

The frontal lobe is associated with executive functions, that is, the ability to organize, make decisions and supervise them. It is where we receive "all" information, process it and proceed from there. Injury to this structure causes irregular behavior, lack of sexual inhibition, and increase in risky behavior.

The parietal lobe is the center of sensory information and plays an important role in language. If injured it can cause dyscalculia (problems with math), dyslexia (problems with language), aphasia (problems with pronunciation), apraxia (problems with movement), and agnosia (problems of recognition).

The temporal lobe, involved in the processes of language related to auditory processing also plays a part in the processing of complex images. Furthermore, it plays a part in the processes of long-term memory consolidation. Injury will cause dyslexia, aphasia and verbal memory impairment.

The occipital lobe is the visual processing center. This is where all the information perceived by sight through the optic nerves goes. Injury to this area causes recognition problems and in the processing of captured images. The localization of areas such as attention, language, or memory indicates the existence of different structures involved in each one of them. Therefore, injury to one of the lobes would result in total or partial loss of said function.

Thus rejecting the locationist theory that ruled the study of neuroscience for decades where they tried to assign a predetermined psychological function to each region of the brain, believing that injury to them prevented the person from developing said functions.

Currently it is believed that cognitive functions are distributed throughout the brain and though there are specialized centers for processing predetermined information, whether they are auditory, visual, or propioceptive; all this will later be distributed to form memory traces.

In order to gain insight into knowledge of the brain we will begin with respects to the emotional world which is more complex than at first sight. We will delve into the different elements that make it up. When we speak about emotional components it depends where we put the focus to say they exist more or less. Therefore, in our first approach we will mention three expressions of emotion:

- Neurophysiologic, comprises all the neural pathways and structures involved particularly in each one of the emotions in addition to the vegetative responses such as vasoconstriction, tachycardia, rapid breathing and skin flushing that accompany emotions.

- Behavioral, in which our body becomes a"mirror" of our emotions, exhibiting them in an involuntary manner through facial expressions and the rest of our body, tensing or relaxing certain muscles, which can give away what we are feeling, even when we are trying to hide it. Likewise, this component tells us what we will or will not do by following that emotion, in other words, how those actions will be expressed in our behavior and in the way in which we relate to others.

- Cognitive has more to do with how we perceive our own emotions and those or others and how we interpret them, in other words, the subjective experience of our feelings.

Lack of adequate emotional education very likely may be behind alexithymia, in which a person is incapable of properly identifying or interpreting their own feelings and those of others.

MacLean (1949) suggested the evolution of the brain in three great stages: reptilian, paleomammalian, and neomammalian; the second one (where the limbic system is located) being the one responsible for emotional processing, which indicates that the emotional system is anterior and would justify its qualities in the processing of affective stimuli.

Regarding the neural network of emotional activity, the areas that are the most involved in the process of emotions are the subcortical (amygdala and basal ganglia) and some cortical areas, primarily the prefrontal cortex, the temporal cortex and the cingulate.

In terms of the location of the processing of positive stimuli versus negative, there has not yet been a consensus. Thus, some authors defend that hemispheric activation takes place equally when exposed to positive and negative stimuli.

Davidson (1984) proposed a model of hemispheric distribution for affective stimuli processing in which the right temporal lobe would process the negative stimuli, while the left would process the positive.

Completing the aforementioned, Heller (1993) postulated the existence of a wider area in the brain (parietotemporal) as the one responsible for analyzing the activating component (arousal) of the stimuli. Thus, the frontal anterior zones would be involved in the processing of valence (positive, negative, neutral) and the emotional experience whereas the posterior zones would process the arousal component and the perceptual aspects of emotions.

The existence of the emotional-perceptual-memory circuit in the human brain is widely agreed on, in which the amygdala plays a crucial role in recording the occurrences of emotional stimuli.

Hence, information with emotional content has significantly more probability to be stored and recovered than information with neutral content.

The extensive connection between the amygdala and the extrastriate visual regions and the hippocampus allows the amygdala to modulate its behavior and facilitate the perceptive and mnesic functions in those areas. These results have been confirmed in patients with injury to the amygdala.

However, there is evidence to indicate that emotional learning associated with the amygdala is temporarily limited and that the subsequent effects on memory may be attributed to the involvement of other regions of the brain such as the orbitofrontal cortex.

We are looking at a circuit of emotional processing that contrasts with the specific cognitive processing pathway. In the emotional circuit the stimuli seem to be automatically analyzed in a rudimentary and rapid fashion, following a configurational strategy. According to Arbib and Fellous (2004) it is a simplified communication, but with high relevance information, necessary for survival and proper development within the ecological niche.

Consequently, this processing ability in parallel

represents a competitive advantage for survival in the environment since it allows the subject to immediately avoid threats and dangers even before this information is consciously evaluated by the prefrontal cortex.

Various animal studies reveal a direct pathway between sensory neurons and the limbic system, particularly to the nucleus of the amygdala.

Alternatively to this pathway, there is a slower and more refined analysis of the stimuli supported by the sensory neurons that connect directly through the nuclei of the thalamus (which also receive information from the amygdala) towards a broad region of the cerebral cortex.

Positron Emission Tomography (PET) studies point to the coexistence of these two different processing pathways. The same results have been obtained through Functional Magnetic Resonance Imaging (FMRI).

It has been observed that the amygdala plays a fundamental role in the processing of emotions. Holland and Gallagher (2004) point out that the amygdala may influence cortical areas in three ways: Those of retro-feeding, stemming from propioceptive signals, visceral and hormonal (which allows the body to prepare for action, whether it is orientation or escape). Those of projection to general activation networks or arousal (putting the body on alert

thus understanding with more clarity threatening stimuli).
And that of the interaction with the medial prefrontal cortex
(which would direct the attentional resources towards the
present emotional stimuli, limiting the rest of the cognitive
processes).

On the other hand, the prefrontal cortex sends different
projections to the amygdala allowing the cognitive functions
(integrators of stimuli process information and its context) to
regulate the role that the amygdala plays in the emotions.

In other words, we respond abruptly (startle and escape
response) at seeing a dangerous animal, for example a bear
(emotional processing) but we do not have the same
response when we see the same bear behind a cage, within
the context of a relaxed Sunday afternoon while visiting the
city zoo with the family (cognitive processing).

Even though up to now we have talked about
specialized areas we must not forget that the brain functions
with electrical and chemical connections, in the latter, the
neurohormones play an important role in emotions.

In addition to the direct innervations between cerebral
structures that establish communication between them by
means of electrical impulses, we have to take into
consideration that there exists a network of connections,
even more difficult to define, thanks to the chemical

substances that function as a means of communication, through what we know as neurohormones such as dopamine, which also have a great influence in perception and emotional expression.

- Dopamine is usually associated with the achievement of pleasure and sexual desire activating the sympathetic nervous system necessary for learning new things based on the desire to attain reinforcement.

High levels improve motivation, disposition, and sexual desire. Suppression causes lack of motivation, indecision, decreased libido, and even depression. Beginning at the vectral tegmentum and reaching the accumbens nucleus, the amygdala, the lateral septal area, the anterior olfactory nucleus, the olfactory tubercle and the neocortex.

- Oxytocin, associated with empathy, sexual desire, and parental behavior, facilitating the development of emotional bonds. It is produced in the supraoptic nucleus and the hypothalamic paraventricular nucleus until it reaches the hypophysis and from there the bloodstream.

- Adrenaline, increases pulse rate and blood pressure and prepares the body for tense situations whether pleasant or not. High levels of adrenaline cause fatigue, lack of attention, insomnia, anxiety, and even depression. Low levels cause listlessness, and depression.

- Norepinephrine, is related to processes of attention, learning, sociability, and sensitivity to the emotions and desires of others. High levels cause mood swings, hypervigilance, and sexual desire. Insufficiency causes lack of concentration, lack of motivation, depression, loss of libido, and social withdrawal.

- Serotonin, associated with appetite, and sexual desire, important in the onset of sleep, blood coagulation, and onset of migraines. High levels cause calm and patience, sociability and adaptability. Deficiency of this neurotransmitter may cause sadness, anxiety, irritability, anger outbursts, hyperactivity, mood swings, insomnia and depression.

- Acetylcholine, affects short term memory. High levels facilitate learning and memory. Suppression causes problems with learning and memory that could lead to senile dementia.

- GABA, gamma aminobutyric acid, responsible for the suppression of a great part of the rest of the neurotransmitters promoting relaxation. High levels cause good memory, sedation, and sleep. Its absence causes difficulty falling asleep, panic attacks, and periods of anxiety.

- Endorphins, belonging to the category of opioid neurotransmitters, regulators of pain, temperature, hunger, and reproduction, also known as the happy hormone. Low levels cause difficulty in feeling pleasure and happiness, and anhedonia, making a person more sensitive to life's setbacks.

Some authors have pointed to the accumulated presence of dopamine and serotonin at the same time as responsible for the onset of anger.

The aforementioned suggests an approximation to the complex web of connections through electrical and chemical pathways of the different structures involved in the formation and maintenance of emotions which the brain has to pay attention to in order to respond for which there exists a series of denominated integrating mechanisms in charge of receiving and analyzing "parts" of information in order to provide the best response.

The primary integrator and the most well know is no doubt the cerebral cortex which receives information from the skin, muscles and sense organs and from there makes either conscious or automatic decisions to maintain balance. Likewise, the allocortex hippocampus and the mesocortex will receive vegetative innervations in additional to emotional information, thus being responsible for producing visceral effects.

Origin of neuropsychological problems

In the field of emotions, not only regarding their structure but also in their behavior, we have to take into account that this is their "normal' development.

But there could be a number of factors that prevent such development from achieving "good performance" as is the case with neurodevelopmental disorders, or once developed these abilities may be lost with the passage of time, especially in the elderly or as a consequence of trauma or illness.

Following, we will show two examples of how abilities and skills may become affected due to modifications "suffered" in the brain.

Keep in mind the close relation between the psychological world and the brain as it happens in the case of trauma. Even though childhood traumas have been the basis for many psychological theories, starting with those of Freud, we still have much to learn about the subject.

One of the limitations of these psychological theories based on childhood traumas is that it is contingent on remembering what happened thirty, forty, or fifty years prior.

As we develop we continually form new "layers" of experiences in life that mold us into who we are and what we do, affecting our present and future decisions.

On occasion we may think that these decisions are not altogether "free" since we can see how they are determined in some way by a traumatic personal experience in the past, whether recent or in childhood.

This is a situation that could be "controlled" by instituting appropriate policies especially in school aged children, thus avoiding that they become victims of attacks by their schoolmates.

Trying to explain the behavior of an adult based on something that happened to them, seems like a very limited proposal. On the other hand, to ignore past events, especially if they were traumatic could be regrettable.

Recent research shows how mistreatment or violence in childhood can leave a "print" in social behavior, confusing and hindering intimate relationships with the opposite sex. But how does childhood trauma affect the brain?

This is precisely what was investigated by a joint study by

The University Hospital Hamburg-Eppendorf, the University of Würzburg, the University Hospital Münster, the University Hospital Johann Wolfgang Goethe-University, the Johannes Gutenberg University Medical Center Mainz, the University Clinic of Würzburg, (Germany) together with the

Karolinska Institutet (Switzerland) whose results have been published in the scientific journal Social Cognitive and Affective Neuroscience Advance Access.

There were 1,158 participants in this study, 325 of which were excluded due to a family history of mental health problems. This left a remainder of 833 adult subjects with an average age of 25.

All were given the standard Childhood Trauma Questionnaire (CTQ) to evaluate traumatic events during their childhood, they were also given the List of Threatening Experiences (LTE) test to evaluate traumatic events within the previous twelve months, the Spielberger Trait Anxiety Inventory (STAI) questionnaire to evaluate the presence of anxiety problems, and the General Depression Scale (CES-D) to verify the presence of depression symptoms, as well as morphological measurements of the brain of 129 of the subjects selected at random.

Results indicate that those who have suffered traumatic events whether recent or in childhood will exhibit significantly more depression and anxiety symptoms than those who have not. The brain morphology study revealed that the anterior cingulate cortex was significantly smaller in these subjects.

In spite of the large number of participants, the study

does not indicate how many of them were male and how many were female. It also does not separate the results into gender categories, which makes it difficult to ascertain if gender plays a role in the consequences of childhood trauma.

Another limitation of the study is precisely the exclusion of 325 of the participants which makes it difficult to learn if or how childhood traumas affect individuals who have a family history of mental health problems.

It is important to emphasize that past and present traumas have emotional effects as well as cerebral. However, the latter do not happen in the amygdala, the center of emotional control as you would expect. Instead, they occur in the anterior cingulate cortex, in charge of, among other things, regulating decision making, empathy, and emotions.

Thus, there is a morphologic alteration that can manifest itself in a change in the way a person relates to others together with depressive symptomatology and anxiety.

Based on these results, childhood traumas must be avoided as much as it is possible since even though they do not determine adult behavior, they do modify the brain and the way it processes emotional information.

Likewise, the brain and cognitive functions may be

affected temporarily or permanently by a trauma or illness as is the case with Parkinson's disease.

When Parkinson's disease is in its advanced stage it is readily recognized by the characteristic tremors, though keeping in mind that not all tremors mean that a person suffers from Parkinson's disease. However, tremors are not the only symptom experienced during the course of this illness, it is also accompanied by sleep disorders, olfactory dysfunction, difficulty walking or moving, change in habits such as speech or writing, and rigidity in expressing emotions.

These symptoms become more readily recognizable as the disease progresses and will worsen existing complications which has a direct effect on the quality of life of the patient and their family since the patient will become increasingly dependent on others and will require almost constant care. There are many observable changes, but there are some psychological in nature that are not that obvious such as mood changes, depression being the most common. Parkinson's disease dementia may also appear in the advanced stages of the disease. This causes memory impairment, affects cognitive problems, language and social behavior. All the aforementioned worsen the quality of life of the patient. But, how does Parkinson's change the brain?

This is precisely what the Universidad de Módena y

Reggio Emilia is trying to study. This study was participated in by 40 individuals, 25 of them were Parkinson's disease patients diagnosed 5 years prior with an average age of 60, and 15 individuals of the same age without the disease.

All were subjected to a functional magnetic resonance imaging (FMRI) procedure where their brain was scanned in search of significant morphological differences between the patients with Parkinson's and the control group.

The researchers found differences in the volume of gray matter in the brain which was particularly reduced in the right parietal cortex and in the internal structure of the brain and in the putamen, responsible for motor skills and the performance of previously learned movements of the patients with Parkinson's.

Two years later the same study was conducted with the same participants to see how their brains had changed with the average age now being 62 years.

They found even more significant differences in the pedunculopontine nucleus and the mesencephalic motor region.

According to the researchers, seeing how the progression of Parkinson's disease affects new areas is great progress as it increases their knowledge on how to treat it. Currently they are developing treatments to stop the progression of the disease and there is even the possibility of eventually reversing the effects of it and thus attain a real cure.

In spite of presenting clear, significant results the study makes it difficult to form a conclusion about the progression of Parkinson's disease since parallel evaluations were not performed about the changes in the disease by means of neuropsychological tests that would determine in which of the five phases it was.

The small number of participants also makes it difficult to extrapolate the results since the effects could have been influenced by the environment where the person grew up, the treatment they received, their diet, etc., uncontrolled variables that would allow the extrapolation of results to other populations of persons affected with Parkinson's disease.

Likewise, the observation of only two years in patients that have suffered for eight years with the disease does not reveal if there were essential differences between the patients to start with.

It is already known that the disease will progress, that the severity of the symptoms will increase and the disability they cause in the patients suffering from Parkinson's. Therefore, the study should continue so as to accompany the patients and observe what new developments are involved in the disease.

Chapter 2 Psychological Processes and their Function

For humans the gestation period is nine months, it is not the longest among mammals, for example, elephants may reach up to twenty-two months. However, there is a distinctive characteristic in our babies with respects to the rest of the animal world and that is they are dependent in order to survive and this extends over a period of several years.

The majority of animals are able to stand on their feet and walk as soon as they are born, or to swim without difficulty if they are aquatic. But, what about humans?

Human babies are one of the most defenseless and dependent, requiring care and attention even beyond puberty before they become independent and self-sufficient; the moment at which they leave home, with a job with which to support themselves, which would be the equivalent of the self-sufficiency of animals, which the majority achieve shortly after they are born whereas in humans this could be prolonged even up until they are thirty years old. Why is this so?

The brain is one of the organs that is not yet fully developed when a baby is born. During the first few years of life it will undergo a series of important changes such as:

- During the fetal stage between the second and fourth month of life the brain undergoes a process of neuronal proliferation followed by one of neuronal selection where apoptosis occurs, in other words, a programmed neuronal death which is survived by only half of the neurons.

After this stage the brain will have this number of neurons for the rest of its life. At least, that was the belief that was held until the discovery of neurogenesis, meaning, the capacity of the brain to form new neurons which can reproduce themselves in an unlimited manner throughout a lifetime including in adult years.

- The process of neural myelination, which consists of covering the neural axons, which is responsible for connecting to other neurons, which facilitates the interconnection between them. This process takes place at different times depending on the region in which it originates. It begins with the primary sensory and motor areas concluding approximately around puberty with the myelination of the frontal and parietal areas.

- The increase of neural connections, facilitated by myelination, has a lot to do with the experiences that a baby undergoes and that will make up the brain. The expression, "Children are like sponges", because they absorb everything, refers precisely to this learning ability   of a brain in development that feeds on all kinds of information coming from its surroundings.

- The increase in brain size, which doubles during the first year of life and triples in the third in relationship to the size of the baby's head when they are born.

- Neuroplasticity, where neurons that were previously indistinct begin to become specialized in the processing of a specific type of information establishing connections with their "neighbors" creating in this way specialized processing regions such as visual, sensitive or motor.

This process of cerebral maturation will continue to occur gradually as the body develops.

However, this development in spite of having plenty of biological programming, in other words, a genetic base that establishes the steps which the brain will take, can be facilitated or hindered with maternal stimulation even during pregnancy. This thought is backed up by a study carried out by the University of Helsinki (Finland) published in the Proceedings of the National Academy of Sciences. They studied thirty three women, half of which were made to listen to a pseudo word, or non-word that was invented and does not exist in their lexicon, while the other half did not listen a to anything new.

After the birth of the babies they were evaluated by administering an electroencephalogram, which records the electrical activity of the brain. They found that the babies in the first group were able to recognize the pseudo words, which indicates a certain ability to learn and memory. The results of this study establish the importance of early stimulation in cognitive development, including before birth during the gestation period.

We designate psychological processes to the different abilities a person has, and even though there is a great interdependence between them we are talk about abilities such as memory, language or attention span, among others.

- Intelligence

The concept of intelligence has been analyzed as unitary and stable at times even though in recent years there has been a theoretic reassessment of its dimensions.

From such has emerged the theory of multiple intelligences, which refers to different dimensions of intelligence, for example, artistic, musical, mathematic, social, etcetera. Based on this, these days a person could have great musical intelligence but not excel in the rest of the intelligences.

The unitary concept of intelligence allows us to speak of

a higher or lower level, but also about an extremely high level (genius) or a limited one. But with the emergence of multiple intelligences a person can be genius in one area but "normal" or even deficient in any other one of the intelligences.

In spite of this change in concept and analysis of the different modalities of intelligence what seems to remain undisputed is the stability of intelligence over time. Notwithstanding, educational institutions go to great lengths to increase this level in their students hoping to somehow improve it by means of education.

But, is the level of intelligence maintained throughout a person's life?

This is what a study conducted by the Western Illinois University and the Loyola Marymount University is trying to prove. The results of said study have been published in the Journal of Intelligence.

The data to be analyzed came from a multivariate, longitudinal study carried out by Murray Research Archive which analyzes participants over a period of 30 years, extracting data from 157 participants when they were 3-4 years of age, 11, 18, and 32.

All of them were given a plethora of standardized questionnaires but the study only used the information related to the Q Methodology and the California Child Q-Set item "High Intellectual Capacity", the development of academic abilities through Wechsler Preschool and Primary Scale of Intelligence (WPPSI). Furthermore, they took into consideration other variables such as sex, and the socioeconomic and education status of their parents. The results show a significant relationship between initial levels of intelligence and those developed over time, evaluated as to their academic performance.

Even though the study is clear about the capability to predict intelligence, it does not go into evaluating the role that education plays on intelligence and whether having a higher or lower education level corresponds with higher or lower intelligence levels. This answer would validate the efforts of the educational institutions or to question them if there is no relation between education level and intelligence.

Likewise the study focuses only on academic intelligence, in other words, the capability to adequately respond to the demands and requirements of academic institutions in each one of the educational levels, forgetting the dimensional approach that takes into consideration that there can be normal academic performance by a normal intelligence in this aspect but then, excel or even be genius in other fields such as artistic, social, etcetera, that only because they are not considered "useful" to the educational institutions they   are neither evaluated nor promote everything that a student may need.

- Language

One of the hardest psychological disorders to determine is the genetic predisposition for language.

The importance of being able to determine the genetic role in these disorders would facilitate the design of precise and effective pharmacological treatments, on the other hand, if the genetic role is minimal or nonexistent then the treatment must be based on psychotherapy except for acute cases where medication could be used for stabilizing the person.

Among genetic alterations that have been found to alter health particularly in the immune system is chromosome 6; in short, in the leukocyte antigens associated with immune disorders present in illnesses such as autism and schizophrenia. But it also points to the possibility that it may affect other disorders in which there is a disruption in linguistic ability not only in comprehension but also in being able to properly speak and be understood as has been observed in children with attention deficit disorder (ADD). Is there a genetic connection to ADD?

This is exactly what is being researched at the University of Oxford, Evelina London Children's Hospital, the University of Edinburgh, the University of Manchester, King's College London, the University of Aberdeen, Tufts University, Max Planck Institute for Psycholinguistics (Netherlands), and Radboud University (Netherlands) recently published in the Journal of Neurodevelopmental Disorders.

The participants of the study were children and families that frequent specialized care centers and children's hospitals. All received a genetic analysis, not including children suffering from autism or any hearing impairment.

They also received three linguistic tests: Nonword Repetition (NWR), Receptive Language Scores (RLS), and Expressive Language Scores (ELS). The last two were performed using the standardized questionnaire Clinical Evaluation of Language Fundamentals (CELF).

The results indicate a significant positive relation between human leukocyte antigens with NWR while this relation is significantly negative with ELS. This means that this genetic makeup will become evident in the linguistic ability of the children that suffer from it. This alteration has been observed more present in children who suffer from ADD. Hence, the speech impediments these children suffer can be explained as an alteration of the genetic makeup.

The results, in spite of being clear in their conclusions only explain a minimal part of ADD. This is a necessary step in explaining the reason but not enough to help understand the psychopathology. It is necessary to also include research related to treatment.

- Memory:

One of the major cognitive problems in life is when the working memory is affected, since this causes great problems when we need to function.

Working memory is that which allows us to work in the here and now remembering what we need to do, following an objective or task.

If our working memory is injured the person can find themselves totally "lost", beginning an activity, such as that of going to buy bread, and halfway there going blank not knowing where they were heading or why

Likewise, in carrying on a conversation this type of memory is necessary to follow to thread of the conversation. When this ability is impaired the person becomes lost and will not know what is being talked about or will repeat the same arguments over and over because they cannot remember having said them before.

Working memory impairment occurs due to the natural aging process of a person as well as due to some psychopathologies as is the case in people suffering from Alzheimer's, but this impairment is also present in young people suffering from ADHD. Thus, some researchers advocate that improving the working memory in children with ADHD will significantly improve their ability to concentrate and in their focused attention helping them to maintain performance levels similar to those of their peers.

As we can see it is very important to know what it entails but above all, if the memory can be adequately trained once it is showing signs that it is failing.

This is exactly what is being researched by a joint study by the University of Oregon, the Louisiana Tech University, the University of California, and the Rose-Hulman Institute of Technology, recently published in the Journal of Behavior and Brain Science,

The study was participated in by 30 youth between 18 and 31 years of age. They were given two evaluations, before and after training.

All the experiments were performed by putting the subject in front of a computer screen while they were asked to perform a task that required the used of their working memory.

The training phase was only participated in by half of the subjects. They were trained for two hours each day during a period of 12 weeks.

At the conclusion of the phases, all the participants, with or without training, went through the evaluation of the transference to check whether there were differences between them.

The results show that there were no differences between the two groups in the first experiment while during the first month of the transference the group that received the specific training showed marked improvement in their working memory.

In addition to the behavioral measures the investigation gathered the electrical activity of the brain showing how the trained participants had greater activity in the   prefrontal areas of the brain exactly where the working memory has been shown to be involved.

Even though the study was carried out with few participants it seems to clearly show the expected benefits of significantly improving the working memory in just 24 hours of training.

Likewise it is still necessary to adapt the materials used to the different populations to which they can be applied, in this way the effective results can be guaranteed in young people as well as the elderly.

The knowledge that with little training such an important and fundamental cognitive ability can be recovered in our day to day with our working memory is a great medical discovery.

- Attention:

Children suffering from ADHD show increased activity at the same time as a decreased attention span. It is important to know which functions are affected in order to adequately treat them.

From a very young age children already display behavior that quickly identifies them as fidgety, unruly and restless, easily distracted in addition to having difficulty learning since they find it hard to keep still and pay attention in class which generally aggravates teachers and even their parents. When this behavior becomes a chronic situation and is sustained with time it may very well be that we are looking at a case of ADD which may or not be accompanied by hyperactivity. In the case of the latter it would be defined as ADHD (attention deficit hyperactive disorder) or ADD (attention deficit disorder without hyperactivity).

ADHD is characterized by impulsive behavior,

interruption of conversations, not letting the other person finish speaking, talking too much, inability to wait their turn whether in speech or in games, constantly getting up, running around, and when sitting, constantly fidgeting or moving their feet.

ADD is characterized by a difficulty paying attention and following instructions, not finishing tasks, lack of organization, often losing their belongings because of not paying attention where they were left, and easily distracted by any noise.

Though the cause of this disorder is not known, it can sometimes "disappear" during the maturation process, though in a small percentage it could go on to adult life. Furthermore, persons who suffer from this begin to develop "coping mechanisms" in such a natural way that they can function normally in both their academic life as well as at work.

In spite of this it can be a source of conflict and an emotional burden on children not only at school but also at home. This is why early detection is fundamental to establish an adequate diagnosis and design a specific treatment that would help to overcome the situation.

ADHD can be categorized in three sub-categories or types: ADHD predominantly inattentive type (ADHD-I),

ADHD predominantly hyperactive-impulsive type (ADHD-H), and ADHD combination type (ADHD-C).

Even though there have been great advances made there are still many "fringes" to understand in ADHD. For example, the role of the central executive as a possible cause to explain inattention.

The central executive associated with the frontal lobes makes reference to the person's ability to establish goals and follow through, design and organize plans, anticipate results, everything opposite what would characterize a child with ADHD-I.

A recent study carried out at East China Normal University (China) And the Kyushu University (Japan) published in the Journal of Behavioral and Brain Science addresses this issue trying to understand the relation between the central executive and ADHD-I.

The study included 16 children diagnosed with ADHD-I who had not received medication three months prior compared with a control group of 21 other children of the same age without any pathology.

The central executive was evaluated in its four different components: planning, working memory, flexibility, and inhibition response; showing a significant difference between the results in children with ADHD and the control group in planning, working memory and inhibition but no difference in flexibility.

This means that children with ADHD-I have a certain immaturity in their central executive since they require more time than the others to establish task planning which in most cases remains unfinished. They also become easily "lost" and "forgetting" what they were doing which makes it difficult for them to carry out their own plans or the instructions of others due to a low performance of their working memory. Lastly, they also exhibit low inhibition which means that any stimuli they are presented with will catch their attention since they have low levels of concentration and for blocking attention to outside stimuli.

This study opens the way to work towards distinguishing, through specific tests, between the different types of ADHD and by these means be able to establish an adapted treatment. Also finding out which areas are deficient in these children will allow the design of concrete therapies to mitigate or compensate for those deficiencies especially in the areas where they show less development of the central executive thereby helping these children to have "normal" activity and be able to perform as the rest of their peers do.

- Emotion:

Emotions have a daily influence in our way of thinking and acting. Therefore, therapy focuses on trying to control them. Since the discovery of PNIE (Psychonueroimmunoendocrinology) which studies the relation between different systems of the body where the psychological has a direct influence in the neural system, the immune system and the endocrine system and continues through all the systems reaching the psychological. After the discoveries by the PNIE system it has been possible to deepen our understanding regarding the origin and treatment of certain conditions, which up to recent years had no clear diagnosis, such as psychosomatic illnesses.

The psychological component is made up of the way of thinking, feeling, and acting which themselves are interrelated. Thus, our way of thinking influences our way of feeling and acting and likewise this happens in the world of emotions and their relation with the other two. But, to what extent can emotions be modified in order to affect the way a person thinks?

This issue is being researched at KU Leuven (Belgium) recently published in the scientific journal Frontiers in Psychology.

The study was carried out on 63 university students who

had to take a standardized test Checklist for Symptoms in Daily Life. In addition, they did not need to have had neither a physical or psychiatric diagnosis nor be taking any medications such as anxyolitics, antidepressants or beta blockers.

Participants were to view images which they had to classify according to their emotions, either positive or negative. In addition to the assigned task, they underwent a cardiac evaluation, and were given a self monitoring questionnaire.

The results indicate a significant change in thoughts when the emotions of the participants were subjected to manipulation.

The administrators highlight the ease with which emotions can change and how quickly they can affect thinking and as a result also affect behavior.

This has a direct application in the field of psychotherapy where the health "tags" can be manipulated, and with that successfully fight psychosomatic illnesses.

Not going to extremes, Viktor Frankl who developed logotherapy, pointed to being able to change someone's life with just a change in dialog which gradually becomes internalized and can change a person's way of thinking.

Regardless of the obvious differences between research work and psychotherapy based on words as is the case with Viktor Frankl the study validates the ideas of the latter since in both cases words, modified in appositive way, can change the way a patient thinks and feels.

- Perception:

We must keep in mind that many of the aforementioned abilities depend largely on external stimuli. It is for this reason that if a person has difficulty with perception this will result in a certain level of handicap when it comes to correctly processing responses to the world around that person.

Today there have been great advances that have been accomplished from engineering and the mechanics to design and invent devices that address specific deficiencies, from crutches, to bionic arms and everything in between such as hearing aids and cochlear implants.

All of these are meant to offer a better "sensory experience" by replacing what is lacking and in that way allowing the person to live as much of a normal life as possible.

Therefore, when we think of deafness, a common problem in older individuals, we tend to think of it as a problem of not much importance. We will see in the following that it does have important emotional implications, since in a society based on communication it seems that deafness can pose more than just an inconvenience.

Loss of hearing is a frequent problem in the elderly, but also among youth who are exposed to very loud sounds, as well as deafness caused by genetics.

Nowadays we are constantly bombarded by sounds coming from different sources such as other vehicles when we are driving, the television showing the news, or another person trying to tell us something.

This is so much so that there are some cities that are considered the noisiest. In these places sometimes it is difficult to separate the noise from the words in a conversation. But, what would happen if we did not have access to that sound?

Many years ago this would have been considered a grave problem but today thanks to medical advances it is considered a problem that can be overcome.

Sign language has allowed people to communicate, to be able to express what one feels, thinks or wants, which otherwise would be an issue that would cause isolation. But what emotional consequences does deafness pose?

This question was researched by the Department of Psychology at the University of Gothenburg (Sweden) whose results were published in the scientific journal Clinical and Experimental Psychology.

There were 53 adults who participated in this study, 33 of them were deaf and the rest had some hearing impairment, 42 were women and the average age was 42 years.

To evaluate the presence of emotional problems they used a standardized scale named Positive Affect Negative and Affect Scale (PANAS). To evaluate levels of stress they used Stress and Energy. And to evaluate levels of self esteem they used Rosenberg's Self-esteem Scale (RSES).

They also gathered sociodemographic data from the participants, level of education, alcohol and tobacco consumption, among other data.

The results show that according to the mental health evaluation following the criteria of the DSM-V, 43% of the participants suffered from major depressive disorder; 33% suffered from anxiety disorder; 33% suffered from stress related traumas; 21.4% had attention deficit disorder (ADD); 12% suffered from obsessive compulsive disorder (OCD); 7% had schyzotypal personality disorder; and 21% autism spectrum disorder; thereby proving that 5% of the participants suffered from substance addiction.

It is important to point out that the sum of the figures of the diagnostics exceeds 100%. The reason is because the same person could suffer from both major depressive disorder and anxiety disorder.

A total of 42% of the deaf participants or those with hearing impairment exhibited more than one psychopathology. Regarding the evaluation of the scales and questionnaires it was concluded that self esteem and energy levels can predict the presence of pathologies associated with emotion.

One of the limitations of the study is in regards to the exposition of the results which make no distinction between those who were deaf and those who only had a hearing impairment.

It would seem as if the more auditory difficulty a person has the more psychological problems would be present but since such a distinction was not made there are no conclusions regarding that.

Also, the criteria of integration that could affect the disposition of the participants was also not taken into consideration. It would seem that integrated deaf people would have fewer psychological problems than those who are not. This is another aspect that also cannot be proven in this study.

In spite of the limitations of the study it has been proven how this collective is especially susceptible to suffer from psychological problems especially those related to the emotional state.

Bearing in mind that the specialized centers for treatment of auditory problems and integration centers should be aware of some of the main symptoms of these psychopathologies so that they could refer their patients to the appropriate health professional when they are detected.

Likewise, it should be expected that they would design prevention programs within this collective so they can have a better quality of life without psychopathological complications.

We must take into consideration too that in spite of having seen these cognitive abilities separately there is a definite interdependency between them.

Chapter 3 Evaluation of Changes in Cognitive Functions

Just as it has been posed in the previous chapter, psychological processes are distributed throughout the brain, and this involves their relocation even though there are defined areas in which they play a substantial role without which there would be "damage" in such areas.

These changes in cognitive functions could stem from an inadequate maturation of the brain as it develops, which would prevent an ability from developing to its full potential, or they could arise from damage occurring at a later time.

The deterioration may be progressive as is the case with age, or due to an illness such as Alzheimer's, or it could appear suddenly such as with cranioencephalic trauma.

In all cases, the suspected affected cognitive function should be evaluated to determine if it, in fact, is damaged or not, and based on the results establish timely treatment

- Changes in intelligence:

A recent study is trying to analyze the difference in existing social skills in children with a dual diagnosis of autism together with Down syndrome.

One of the most important challenges facing pediatricians and parents is being able to recognize if the child is developing normally or not in comparison to other children of the same age.

There could be many circumstances that can cause dysfunctions in the development of a child, some resolve themselves as the child grows, and others require therapy by specialists not only for the diagnosis but also for the treatment.

If in addition to the dysfunction, whether it is in motor, intellectual, or communication skills, there are also characteristic physical traits this could help to indicate whether we are dealing with a child with Down syndrome. This diagnosis can be quickly made since in addition to its visible physical characteristics there is the presence of a genetic alteration in the chromosome 21 pair, where there is an extra chromosome found. This is also known as Trisomy 21.

The fact that this type of chromosomic alteration is accompanied by all its physical and developmental consequences does not necessarily mean that the same relative percentage of a population does not suffer from other types of dysfunctions or disorders whether they are developmental or of another type.

The challenge lies precisely in being able to distinguish which symptoms belong to Down syndrome and which belong to another, especially when it affects development where its main characteristic is precisely a slowing down of the development of motor skills, language, cognitive ability, and emotional control, using as reference children of the same age. But is it possible to find a child affected with autism and Down syndrome at the same time?

This is specifically what is being studied by the Hospital Alto Deba (Spain), Hospital Donostia (Spain), and the Fundación CITA - Alzheimer Fundazioa (Spain) whose results have been published in the Journal of Neurodevelopmental Disorders.

As has already been expressed in the introduction, the difficulty in detecting both disorders at the same time lies in knowing how to distinguish to which of the two the symptoms the children are exhibiting correspond to.

In the case of Down syndrome, a child may exhibit a certain delay in the development of language and social skills in addition to the typical physical characteristics which could be completely overlooked since they would also display a delay in the development of other skills as well, this situation may cover up the fact that the child also suffers from autism spectrum disorder.

This second diagnosis is so complex that the authors of the study claim that there are no statistics to date that show both disorders present at the same time. In spite of that, they designed a study to try to distinguish the symptoms of one from the other.

The study had 46 participants between the ages of to 21 years, 26 female and 20 male all being diagnosed with Trisomy 21, or Down syndrome and they were specifically chosen because none had been diagnosed with autism spectrum disorder.

All were given a series of questionnaires such as the Social Responsiveness Scale (SRS) in which the caretakers evaluate the level of social involvement of the children. They were also given the Social Communication Questionnaire (SCQ). In order to determine the social performance through non-verbal language they used the Leiter International Performance Scale-Revised (Leiter-R), and the Peabody Picture Vocabulary Test, Fourth Edition (PPVT-4).

When someone passes a test designed for autism spectrum disorder patients who does not suffer from the illness helps to figure out which items and scales of the test will be shown in the population of those diagnosed with Down syndrome and which will not be shown.

It is the latter who will help to establish a diagnosis in the new cases since, if present, they will show that they also suffer from autism spectrum disorder.

The most remarkable results show significant results in two subscales of the SRS test, specifically in the areas having to do with social cognition and mannerisms, the latter being repetitive movements such as rocking.   According to the authors of the study these are the most important symptoms to keep in mind when it is time to evaluate the presence of autism spectrum disorder in children with Down syndrome.

The study has such a small number of participants and the age range is so wide that it is necessary to conduct another investigation with more subjects in order to arrive at a valid conclusion.

Likewise, the minimum age of the participants is 10 years which does not help in using the study as a useful diagnostic tool since the earlier it is detected, the sooner that there can be an intervention.

- Changes in Language:

When we think about Alzheimer's we tend to think only about memory problems, but these are not the only symptoms that occur during the first stages of the disease that need to be addressed.

It is true that the first symptoms of Alzheimer's are generally mistaken with those arising from the passing of time especially when these occur in advanced age but there are tools especially designed for detecting its symptoms not only through means of observation of external symptoms, but also through implementation tasks.

All this data is compared to previous population group results, in other words with "normal" population, to confirm if the person has symptoms appropriate for their age or if they are due to other factors that need to be further investigated.

A more detailed analysis helps to corroborate or discard an Alzheimer's diagnosis

The problem lies in that the symptoms of the disease in its early stages are so minor that they do not cause discomfort to the patient or "complaints" by their family and so rarely do they feel the need to see a specialist for a checkup.

Among these symptoms are those related to speech, which is characteristically affected by Alzheimer's by difficulty following a conversation, using superficial facts and few details, constant mistakes when making references to the past, interruptions in the thread of the conversation, repetitions, circumlocution (saying too many things going around a main idea), and repeating themselves.

This symptomatology although not exclusive to

Alzheimer's patients does influence the quality of their relationships, due to the fact that they cannot maintain an adequate level of communication. This causes the conversation partners to lose interest in talking to someone who is not capable of responding adequately, this further promotes the isolation of the patient. But, is it possible to improve these first symptoms of Alzheimer's?

The University of Nebraska Omaha and the University of South Alabama have been collaborating in the research on this subject. The results have been published in the International Journal of Alzheimer's Disease.

The study included 5 adults that had more than five years suffering from Alzheimer's with a score of between 5 and 6 on the Global Deterioration Scale (GDS). All the patients showed difficulty in speech according to the results from the standardized test Arizona Battery of Communication Disorders of Dementia (ABCD).

The tests were carried out in 20 minute sessions in a context of conversation so that:

- The relevant ideas of the conversation were emphasized.

- There were yes/no questions in order to restructure the sentences.

- The missing information was indicated at the same time as the main idea of the conversation was emphasized.

- Words or phrases that did not belong were indicated so they would be eliminated.

All the above was emphasized with gestures.

The results compared between the data of coherence obtained from Glosser and Deser and the Healthy Elderly (HE) before and after therapy show remarkable improvement regarding speech, not only in quality but also in fluency.

This design, in spite of showing significant results, lacks a comparison control group. This detail could possibly render the results invalid since the pre and post evaluations are affected by a non-controlled variable.

The study uses a small number of participants. Therefore, the conclusions, however clear they may be, need to be corroborated by new investigations including a larger number of subjects.

Also it bears keeping in mind that this therapy is given to alleviate the symptoms caused by Alzheimer's and not necessarily an attempt at trying to find some type of cure. That is to say, this therapy on its own will not stop the progression of the disease. In order to do that, it would need to be applied in conjunction with other therapies including psychopharmacology.

In spite of the previously mentioned items, a therapy such as the one hereby analyzed can do much to correct the first symptoms of Alzheimer's offering with it better quality of life for longer time for the patient thereby helping the patient to maintain a normal level of communication with their family and friends.

Techniques could be used that are very similar to those used in children with delayed development, such as autism. These techniques have been used over the years with great results.

Once the limitations of the study that have been brought out are overcome there can be a simple and easy therapy design that can be learned in rehabilitation centers for family members so they can use this in their own homes with the patient and thus optimize therapy.

- Changes in Memory:

Autism spectrum disorder affects many abilities, the main one being communication skills.

Autism spectrum disorder is a disruption in development that prevents children from acquiring the skills and abilities appropriate for their age causing a delay in development as compared to their peers.

This delay will be sustained over time including up to adulthood if there are no corrective therapies applied n a timely manner.

The main focus of the investigation is childhood as the critical moment in which to detect the first symptoms of ASD as well as for designing and implementing therapy programs aimed at reinforcing the development of communication skills and thus correct impairments that could arise.

However, there is still investigation being carried out to try to understand how this disorder will affect the patient for the rest of their lives.

As it has been mentioned previously, it is expected that if something has not developed properly during childhood, whether it is communication skills or something else, you would expect to see these same problems during adult life. Can adult autism patients suffer from memory problems?

This is exactly what is being researched at the University of London whose results have been published in Autism Research.

This study involved 36 individuals, 9 women and 27 men

between 20 and 62 years of age. Half of them were diagnosed with autism spectrum disorder, the other half were the control group who had a "normal" development.

All the participants were subjected to an evaluation of their verbal development using the standardized tests Verbal Intelligence Quotient (VIQ), Performance Intelligence Quotient (PIQ), Full Scale Intelligence Quotient (FSIQ); and an intelligence test using the Wechsler Adult Intelligence Scale (WAIS).

The group of patients with autism spectrum disorder was further reevaluated with the Autism Diagnostic Observation Schedule (ADOS). All the participants had to undergo tests on a computer where they were shown a series of stimuli and they were required to respond according to the instructions of the test.

The results show poor performance by the patients with autism spectrum disorder compared with the control group in all the memory tests given.

Also, there was a progressive diminishing of performance in the memory tests of the control group as their age increased, worsening correspondingly.

This change is not apparent in the patients with the autism spectrum disorder diagnosis. It seems there is an equalizing of the results of the advanced age group with the results of the patients with autism spectrum disorder.

This information can help in developing therapy programs to strengthen memory strategies including in adults with autism spectrum disorder since if the impairments are not corrected, they will continue through time.

Keep in mind however, that these results were obtained in an "artificial" environment such as a behavioral lab where memory skills are tested in a very clinical way, knowing that in "normal" life a person gets more clues, for example through notes, which could compensate where memory fails thus allowing the person to carry out their life like everyone else.

It bears reiterating that there is a great disproportion in the number of participating women which calls for the need to carry out new investigations that take into consideration gender differences before drawing conclusions on the matter.

- Changes in attention:

One of the biggest concerns for parents of children with ADHD is knowing whether or how this will affect their future. Many questions arise, not only about treatment but also about whether there will be future repercussions or consequences.

Literature on the subject of adult ADHD shows that they are more likely to suffer from depression or anxiety together with impairment with quality social relationships, their health and self esteem. These are phenomena that are not very well understood. Therefore, the importance of continuing to study them.

It also shows how disorders present during childhood and even in infancy can disappear with time due to the maturing process of the brain that allows it to correct existing impairments.

One of the phenomena that is well known in regards to attention is facilitation and suppression.

- With the correct code there is a reduction in response time since the brain can accurately anticipate a response given the facilitation.

- With the incorrect code there is an increase in response time since the brain anticipates an incorrect solution that needs rectification, further slowing down the process giving way to suppression. But what happens with adults with ADHD? Would they conduct themselves with the same attentional codes?

To answer this question Hampshire College conducted a study in which the consequences of ADHD on adults are analyzed.

In this study there were 25 adults diagnosed with ADHD compared to a control group of 25 adults without any psychopathology.

To avoid the effects that medication would have on the ADHD patients, the test was performed a minimum of 18 hours after taking them in order to rule out any ADHD medication enhancing effect or interference.

The experiment consists in the response to an attentional task where the participants were shown arrows on the screen pointing to where the stimulus would be to be selected as quickly as possible with the chance that there would appear a distracter or signal that was not to be answered. Their electrical brain activity was being recorded while they were taking the test.

The data shows "normal"performance in both groups in facilitation as well as in suppression in attentional tasks not only in its execution but also in the electrical brain activity.

In children with ADHD there was a definite deficit of attention.

This supports the idea that the maturing process does

have a strong correcting role, at least for some tasks, with ADHD not having consequences in the life of an adult.

- Changes in Emotion:

On occasion we know more about and illness because of the symptoms appearing in its advanced stages as is the case with Parkinson's disease.

Parkinson's is a neurodegenerative disease that becomes progressively worse with time. Starting with Stage I with tremor and other movement symptoms occur on one side of the body only possibly dragging the feet and showing symptoms of stiffness. In Stage II the person begins to stoop forward, begins to have trouble with balance and difficulty initiating movements (bradykinesia). In Stages III and IV symptoms worsen affecting balance and making it difficult to walk. In Stage V, the final stage, the person needs constant care by a third party for all daily activities. During this stage the person spends most of his or her time sitting or lying down due to the constant tremors.

As the illness progresses options for treatment of Parkinson's become increasingly limited starting with pharmacological and rehabilitative treatment up to surgical. Of the latter types of treatment there are those that are reversible such as deep brain stimulation (DBS) and those that are irreversible including surgery which targets certain areas of the brain.

Among these surgical procedures is a palidotomy, which is the most common, where an incision is made in the globus pallidus of the brain. This procedure has been found to have emotional consequences on patients. Do surgical procedures in the brain of a Parkinson's patient bring about emotional changes?

There is recent research on this subject being carried out by the Hospital de Santa María (Portugal) published recently in the scientific journal Parkinsonism & Related Disorders.

The study had 30 participants who underwent a surgical procedure to treat the advanced stages of Parkinson's.

All participants had a previous study and monitoring for a year following the procedure where they were given a standardized test to detect emotions called Comprehensive Affect Testing System (CATS) in which seven basic emotions are evaluated in facial recognition tasks and four based on language (prosody). Results show that there are no significant changes between the data obtained before or after the surgical procedure.

Before the procedure they had observed apathy and depression in 6 of the patients, later that number rose to 14 a year after the procedure. These findings no doubt need to be studied to find out why the number of persons with depression doubled a year after the procedure and if this is a "normal" development of the illness or a product of the surgery.

Lack of studies underscore that there was not a control group to compare the development of the illness over the course of time, neither was an exhaustive evaluation carried out about the state of mind of the patient neither before nor after the surgical procedure.

Due to the limitations of the study it is hard to generalize the results until the number of patients is increased, there is a control group, and the development of the state of mind of the patients who received a surgical procedure is analyzed as a means to face the most advanced stage of Parkinson's disease.

- Changes in Perception:

One of the biggest challenges for children with autism is social integration. Is there a relation between deafness and autism?

This question is closely related to the social and integration skills of the child since if the child is deaf it would be difficult for him or her to hear what others are saying thereby making it difficult to offer a response.

This has motivated researchers to try to solve the problems associated with such disorder. This would improve the quality of life of the child.

The type of hearing impairment that has important implications in the development of any child and that could be addressed with early detection could be easily overlooked in the children with autism spectrum disorder due to the fact that there are "more serious" problems to deal with.

Although if you ask parents and even the specialists who are well versed on this subject it is usually quite the opposite, in other words, one of the characteristics of autism spectrum disorder is hyper sensibility, to touch, taste, and even sound.

These children do not know how to react adequately and are bothered by sudden, unexpected, repetitive, or loud sounds such as an alarm, a washer, or an ambulance siren. Is there a relation between deafness and autism?

This subject is being researched by the Department of Hearing and Speech Sciences, Faculty of Allied Health Sciences, Health Sciences Center, Kuwait University (Kuwait) whose results were published in the scientific journal Communication Disorders, Deaf Studies & Hearing Aids.

The study was carried out with 22 children all males ages 7 to 15 and diagnosed with autism spectrum disorder.

All were given two hearing tests, one was the Transient Otoacoustic Emissions (TOAEs) to evaluate the integrity of the cochlea and the ciliated cells; and the other was a tympanometry which evaluates the middle ear.

Results show that 17 of the boys, or 77%, exhibited reduced hearing ability.

Not including girls in the study makes it impossible to see if there is a difference in the relation of deafness to autism based on gender.

One of the limitations of the study is the small number of participants. This makes it impossible to extrapolate the relation between deafness and autism until there is new research.

By not applying traditional hearing problem measuring means based on the person's behavioral response it cannot be concluded if these new methods are more effective or not.

It is important to note that the study focused on a problem that is rarely addressed since parent attribute this lack of auditory attention to traits common to autism spectrum disorder and not to a separate issue as such.

If new research presents information similar to such a high number as 77% of relation of deafness to autism, then it would be necessary to consider giving hearing tests to all children with autism spectrum disorder.

In any case, and as the authors of the study recommend, families that have doubts in this regard should visit an ear nose and throat doctor (otorhinolaryngologist) to rule out hearing problems in their children such as deafness which no doubt is an added problem to the existing developmental disorder.

Early detection is important in order to increase the possibilities for improvement therapies for the child. This aspect can be easily corrected with the current scientific advances, whether it is carried out through the reinforcing of hearing activities or even with the use of devices.

There are many standardized test that have been designed to evaluate cognitive functions listed as follows:

- BRIEF-P Behavior Rating Inventory of Executive Function- Preschool Version

Evaluation of executive functions used by parents and teachers to rate children ages 2 to 5.

- SART-R Sustained Attention to Response Task – Revised

Evaluation to sustained attention through a CPT type

monitoring task.

- ICAP Intensive comprehensive aphasia program

An intensive, comprehensive group aphasia treatment program.

- SCIP Screen for Cognitive Impairment in Psychiatry

A simple and easy to administer scale developed for screening cognitive deficits that are most common in adults with some form of psychiatric impairment: memory, attention, executive functions and processing speed.

- CAPA Child and Adolescent Psychiatric Assessment Evaluation of the main emotional problems and behavior of children and adolescents.

- CUMANES (Spain) School Aged Children Neurological Maturity Questionnaire

Global evaluation for the neuropsychological development and cognitive performance of children

- CUMANIN (Spain) Child Neuropsychological Maturity Questionnaire

Integrated system for the investigation of the level of neurological maturity in preschool children evaluating the four basic mental functions: Language, Memory, Motor skills, and Sensoriality by means of 13 scales.

- ENFEN (Spain) Neurological Evaluation of Executive Function in Children

Evaluation of the maturity level and cognitive performance in activities related with executive function in children.

- LNNB Luria-Nebraska Neuropsychological Battery for Adults

Neuropsychological exam for the higher cortical processes (Language, Memory, Attention and Visual- Spatial Functions) and their disorders following the Luria model.

- LNNBCR Luria-Nebraska Neuropsychological Battery – Children's Revision

Evaluation of the executive and linguistic performance, processing speed, and immediate memory in young children following the Luria model.

- MMSE Mini-Mental State Examination

Questionnaire used extensively in clinical and research settings to measure cognitive functions and mental state in adults.

- ANILLAS (Spain) Test for the Evaluation of Executive Functions

Evaluation of the executive function performance in

adults though the ability to plan.

- CAMDEX-R. Cambridge Mental Disorders of the Elderly Examination – Revised.

Accurate clinical diagnostic assessment of the most common types of dementia, as well as other mental disorders.

- FDT Five Digit Test

Evaluation of the cognitive processing speed and specific aspects of attention and the executive functions such as attention control, alternation, and resistance to distraction.

- MFF Matching Familiar Figures Test

Evaluation of the cognitive, reflexive or impulsive tempo of children's reaction to complex tasks,

- SDMT Symbol Digit Modalities Test

Quick detection of cognitive dysfunctions in children and adults by means of a classic task of substituting symbols with numbers. It is one of the screening tests used for the evaluation of cognitive symptoms in patients with multiple sclerosis.

- SCWT Stroop Color and Word Test

One of the most extensively used tests to assess

neuropsychological problems, brain damage and evaluate cognitive interference.

- WCST Wisconsin Card Sorting Test

Neuropsychological evaluation of the various components of executive function, such as abstract reasoning, conceptualization skills, problem solving and perseveration.

- BENDER Bender Visual-Motor Gestalt Test

Assessment of the maturation level in impaired children and adults who have lost functions and of organic brain defects in adults and children as well as personality disorders especially those of regression.

- BRIEF-2 Behavior Rating Inventory of Executive Function – by parents and teachers

- CAMDEX-DS Cambridge Examination for Mental Disorders of Older People with Down's syndrome and others with intellectual disabilities

Assessment of the most common types of dementia as well as other mental and physical disorders present in adults with Down's syndrome or another form of intellectual disability.

- FROSTIG Developmental Test of Visual Perception

Test for the evaluation of delays in perceptive maturity in children with learning disabilities. Evaluates the following aspects of visual perception: Eye motor coordination, Figure ground, Constancy of shape, Position in space, and Spatial relationships.

- HARRIS. Test of Lateral Dominance

Evaluation of patterns of hand, foot and eye dominance which is a relevant aspect in reading and writing difficulties.

- HPL Tests of Uniformity and Lateral Preference

Assessment of uniformity and lateral dominance of the hand, eye and foot. Important in the study of people with difficulty with written or spoken language, motor skills or spatial orientation problems.

- PMT Porteus Maze Test

Psychological test designed to measure psychological planning capacity and foresight which are components of the executive function and are related to social adaptation

- ROFC Rey-Osterrieth Complex Figure

Clinically useful test commonly used in neuropsychology for the evaluation of visuospatial abilities, eyemotor coordination and visuospatial memory.,

- TESEN (Spain) Test of Trails for the Evaluation of

Executive Function (TMT)

Evaluation of performance of the executive function in adolescents and adults by means of a planning task consisting of an eyemotor activity. (Trail Making Test).

- TIDA. Daltonism or Color Blindness Test

Detection and diagnosis of the anomalies in color vision such as Daltonism, color blindness and achromatopsia

- BVRT Benton Visual Retention Test

Examination of visual perception and visual memory. Diagnostic of anomalies in the area of brain pathology and assessment of premorbid level of intelligence affected by organic defect.

Keep in mind this evaluation is accompanied by neuroimaging so the affected areas can be easily seen especially in the case of brain damage.

Brain damage can be due to cranioencephalic trauma, vascular brain accidents (ictus), brain tumors and others.

Likewise these neuroimaging techniques help to ascertain to which extent the trained functions supplant the deficiencies shown in previous evaluations and in this way verify the success of the therapy.

Chapter 4 Psychological Processes Therapy Techniques

Neuropsychology has many applications, whether it is strictly in the clinical field or in others such as educational. Neuropsychology helps us to know who is "meant for school"or to anticipate impairments early in order to intervene.

We would all like our children to be President of a country or a company, an astronaut, or doctor, in other words, to go as far as possible in their professional careers. Or maybe we would like them to accomplish what we could not. Perhaps we would want them to be what we are and accomplish the same things we already have. But how much of that is realistic?

Regardless of what we want, the child will go through different phases in his life and we can be a decisive influence in some of them, especially when they are young, taking them to private academies, motivating them and encouraging them towards that which we think "is best for their future". But as they grow older our ability to "influence" them decreases as they begin to have their own opinions or are influenced by their friends which will be critical when it comes to making decisions about their education and as a result which direction their professional life will take. Does that guarantee their success in the future?

For years some governments have developed population screening policies in which all children have to undergo a series of approved questionnaires in order to "detect" those who have the greatest potential for a field or another and by means of this offer better guidance. We find a history of this in the classic intelligence questionnaires.

Early detection and proper orientation, whether it is by the public institutions or by the parents, helps to know what field the child will be best at and what subjects would best to teach him. However, the final decision will always rest with the child since it is he who will have to make the effort to achieve these future goals. What determines the performance in these different tests? Is it possible to predict in advance the professional future of the children?

With this background information a group at the Karolinska Institutet (Sweden) has conducted a study published in the Journal of Neuroscience where they have tried to answer the aforementioned questions taking into account only the working memory, which is the capacity to retain and manage short term memory.

Working memory has been shown to be a good predictor of better performance with time, not only in mathematics but also in reading. Therefore, a child with limited development of his working memory capacity will display difficulties in the future. This working group has been the subject of studies, using MRI with the goal of establishing a useful method for early detection in children at risk of suffering limited cognitive development.

There were 232 participants in this study between the ages of 6 and 20. The patients diagnosed with ADD or dyslexia by means of a technique for neuropsychological evaluation adapted for each age was excluded. They were given a working memory test that cannot be evaluated directly but only seeing the results in the performance of a task. They also made use of Raven's Progressive Matrices (RPM) to measure their reasoning ability.

The same participants had to undergo the same tests two years later to evaluate the consistency of the measures or the change in them with time.

Results show two structures that are involved in a better prediction of the performance of tasks involving working memory and with this a better future academic and professional development. These structures were the thalamus and the caudate nucleus.

This helped the investigators to conclude that MRI can be used as an evaluation tool for early detection of delayed development of these structures in children and thereby intervene, since not doing so would put their cognitive development and with that, their academic and professional future at risk.

Psychological processes depend on many factors:

- Age of the patient; understanding that the younger they are the greater chance they have to develop those impaired psychological processes.

- Number of affected processes; it is not the same to treat a single problem than treating a patient that has a number of psychological processes affected.

- The severity of the condition; if it is mild, therapy will shorter and more successful.

- Time elapsed between the onset of the "problem" and when therapy begins. Knowing that the more time that passes between the two diminishes the rate of success.

It is important to understand that therapy should always be administered by mental health professionals and whenever possible in an adequately equipped facility for such therapies.

There are two types of therapies to reach this objective:

- Neuropsychological stimulation; which refers to therapies for developing skills and abilities not currently present in the patient and that because of their age should be present. This type of therapy is mainly used in children with cognitive development delays.

- Neuropsychological rehabilitation; is concerned with the amelioration of cognitive, emotional, psychosocial and behavioral deficits caused by age, injury or disease and it is generally administered to older patients or patients with a diagnosed mental illness.

We must keep in mind that cognitive delays are generally accompanied in some cases by other maturation delays, for example in movement, as we will see in the following in the case of autism spectrum disorder:

As we have seen previously early intervention is crucial being that what is accomplished during this phase will determine in a large measure the future quality of life of the child.

It is important to recognize that during this stage in infancy is where children can acquire new skills and cognitive development more easily since their brain has not yet completed the maturation process therefore it is more impressionable or plastic and responds well to neuropsychological interventions.

Child language development is one of the most researched subjects in Developmental Psychology to see how it can be improved.

This is a fundamental element when we consider that some children exhibit problems in their language development. Therefore, it is important to study and analyze it in addition to establish training and improvement programs for those who exhibit these delays in comparison to children their own age.

One of the first challenges a child faces in the development of language is determining the specifics of it, in other words, distinguishing words as single sounds within a continuous dialog.

This is the same difficulty experienced by adults trying to learn a new language. They could listen to it over and over again and still not be able to discern when a word ends and another begins since in normal speech words are linked together so it sounds as if it was a continuous train of sounds with barely an interruption.

All we have to do is remember the first time we heard a foreign language, maybe Chinese, or German or any other. There is the feeling of not knowing what is being said in terms of meaning and also not understanding the individual words that are being spoken.

As we develop our ear we begin to be able to identify the few words we know the meaning of within a phrase and also those we do not know. This ability is due to language development which enables us to identify sounds and to space them appropriately. This happens gradually as we develop a greater vocabulary in that new language and thus it becomes increasingly easier to   listen to and understand longer and more complex phrases.

The phase of language command occurs when we are able to hear each sound separately and identify the meaning, not only of individual words but also of complete phrases, something that with time and practice becomes automatic, so much so that we no longer have to put much effort to understand that language that at first was so difficult to learn.

This language development skill is called segmentation and is what allows us to identify the boundaries between words. This preliminary is necessary before we can begin to identify subject, verb and other parts of speech. Studies show that this process can begin in children as young as 10 months of age depending on the language in which the study is conducted. Is it possible to improve the language development in a child?

This subject is being researched by the Max Planck Institute for Psycholinguistics, the Utrecht University (Netherlands), Radboud University Nijmegen and the University of Amsterdam (Netherlands), and the Western Sidney University (Australia), published recently in the scientific journal Brain Science.

There were two studies conducted to analyze the development of child language. In the first one there were 15 girls and 13 boys, 10 months old, who were administered auditory stimuli and were evaluated 6 months later to determine whether they could recall the sounds using a test for familiar sound identification together with recording brain activity. The results showed significant improvement compared to the control group who had not received the stimulation.

The same test was given to the children at 5 years of age to determine whether they maintained the original improvement when they were exposed to a language different than theirs, this time by means of a standardized questionnaire called Reynell Developmental Language Scales. The results showed no significant observable difference in the children with early exposure to the new language in comparison to the control group.

The investigators point out that there needs to be a distinction between positive effects of early influence of other languages and the effect of the course of time that causes all of us, children and adults, to gradually forget something we are not using. For example, if we learn French at school and we never use it again, it is very likely that 5 years later it will be very difficult to recognize the words in a normal conversation.

However, among the limitations of the study are the small number of participants and that the new language though possessing different linguistic roots is relatively accessible due to the geographical proximity of the participants involved in the study

Likewise, the effect of the course of time is confused with the possibility of lack of language development. It would be necessary to observe if this early exposure that had such great results in the beginning could be used to make it easier for these children that were exposed to the language at an early age to learn such language quicker than the children their age who were not exposed to it at such an early age.

As we can see therapy is possible and effective when we know which variable will play a role in such process.

Conclusions

The field of study of Psychology encompasses any human activity to understand how it comes about and what influence it can have on a person's life. Hence, the inclusion of an activity that is becoming ever more frequent in adults as well as adolescents which is the extensive and intensive use of the internet, especially the use of social media.

About Juan Moisés de la Serna

Doctor of Psychology, Master in Neuroscience and Behavioral Biology, Clinical Hypnosis Specialist. Recognized by the International Biographical Center (Cambridge – UK) as one of the top one hundred health professionals in the world in 2010. He also teaches in various national and international universities.

Scientific disseminator participating in congresses, conferences and seminars; collaborator in various papers, digital media and radio programs; author of the blog "Cátedra Abierta de Psicología y Neurociencias" [Open Chair on Psychology and Neurosciences], and seventeen books on diverse themes.

Currently he conducts research in the field of Big Data in healthcare utilizing data from India, United States and Canada, among others, work which he complements with consultancy to technological startups geared towards psychology and personal wellbeing.

TAIJI BOOK CONTENTS

A Taste of China in Winchester, Virginia, USA

Guests at Open Door School

Other Organizations, Events, and Teachers

Other Influences

ABOUT THIS BOOK

This book is intended to offer supplemental information for students of the Chinese martial and energetic health arts of Taijiquan (also spelled Taiji or Tai Chi) and Qigong (sometimes spelled Chi Kung) as well as some related topics. It is not an instruction manual for beginners or a "how to" guide for specific exercises. It does contain a collection of practical and philosophical information that is not always presented in typical classes. I've been fortunate to have been exposed to many knowledgeable teachers that shared their wisdom. I'll share some brief stories of my interactions with these experts as well as some biographical information about them. It is my hope that students of these arts will find at least one new piece of useful information within. I apologize to everyone for my amateurish attempt to put together this book.

Jan Gyomber, PhD

A NOTE ABOUT ROMANIZATION AND CHINESE NAMES

Taijiquan and Qigong are Chinese arts. There are two main systems of romanization (translation into the Latin alphabet for western languages). Taijiquan and Qigong are the common modern Pinyin system spellings of these arts. The old Wade Giles method usually spelled them as Tai Chi Chuan and Chi Kung. There were usually also diacritical marks used to indicate pronunciation. To add to the confusion, the art of Taijiquan is often shortened to Taiji, and Tai Chi Chuan to Tai Chi.

Chinese names are often written with the family name first. Many Chinese westernize their names when moving to other countries, putting their family names last. They sometimes choose a western first name to fit in better and ease pronunciation struggles for their new neighbors.

In this book I will often use "Taiji" when discussing the martial art and "Qigong" when discussing the energy art. Occasionally I will use other spellings if a teacher used them in their writings. I will usually use the version of their name that was used when we met.

INTRODUCTION

Lucky. Not how I thought of myself for most of my life, although I now think I've been luckier than many. Many doors of opportunity were opened for me, but I often entered only when pushed from behind by others. I now thank them.

When conversing with friends, family, or students, I have often been told "You should write a book." Although unsure if access to accumulated stories and information was wanted, or if folks just wanted me to stop talking, I started jotting down some thoughts. Realizing that there are now many books available on the subjects of Taijiquan and Qigong, I've decided to focus on unique pieces of information or unique approaches to familiar topics gleaned from personal interactions with experts in these fields. This is not a generalized introduction to these arts, but a collection of tidbits that may help fill in some informational gaps for curious students.

Though not a formal student of Dr. Yang Jwing-Ming, I've attended a few dozen of his seminars, and had some friendly conversations with him. He has expressed his concern that authentic Taijiquan was fading in China in favor of either a simplified exercise version, or an extreme, gymnastic-style designed for competition performance. He wanted to encourage practitioners to study, maintain, and pass on genuine, traditional Taijiquan wisdom. Dr. Yang often told those training with him not to believe him, but to ponder his advice, try to incorporate it, and then decide if it was valuable enough to keep and teach. In that spirit, I humbly attempt to pass on what I have learned.

Many people have shared their thoughts, wisdom, and encouragement with me, sometimes in large classes, sometimes in personal instruction sessions, and occasionally during casual conversations. Some of these folks are close friends, some friendly but not close, some might not even remember me, although they had a significant influence. The information in this book is based on my interpretation of lessons conveyed to me by these various experts. Unfortunately, I took very few written notes, and most of those have been lost. I admit that the accuracy of both my memories and interpretations may be less than perfect. Any quotes should be read as paraphrases. Wanting to pass on these accumulated lessons, I tried my best to be true to the teachings. I apologize in advance to any and all that I may have misunderstood. The wisdom is theirs, the mistakes are mine.

To my teachers, thank you. To my Taiji brothers and sisters, thank you. To all my students, thank you. I've learned much from you, and from trying to pass on what I have learned.

MY PATH TO TAIJIQUAN AND RELATED ARTS

During my first two years of primary school, I was the smallest kid in my class. At first that wasn't a problem, but eventually bigger and older kids tried to establish their dominance by picking on me. When I came home with scrapes or a bloody nose my mother wanted to talk to the teachers or parents of the bullies. My father had different ideas. "The way to deal with bullies is to stand up to them. They don't like to get hit either, so fight back as hard as you can and don't stop." Armed with this questionable advice I was determined to fight back the next time I was bullied. Meanwhile I was learning a little about fighting by tussling with my bigger, older, future football all-star and U.S. Marine brother, Mike.

The next time I was bullied I fought back. I ended up on the ground with a bloody nose, but when my tormentor turned to walk away victoriously, I got up, ran after him and jumped on his back. He threw me on the ground again. I got up and charged him again. "What is the matter with you? Stay down!" he ordered as he knocked me down again. When he turned away, I grabbed his leg. "Get off of me!" he shouted in frustration. "Leave me alone!" Now it was my turn. From the ground I demanded, "Say uncle! Admit that I won!" He responded "Okay, okay you won. Now let go of my leg."

Similar scenarios played out through primary school and into junior high as I gradually got better at defending myself and most of the bullies realized I was more trouble than I was worth. Surprisingly, some of those tormentors became my protectors when new bullies showed up. It was a good thing to hear a former nemesis say in my defense "Leave the kid alone or you'll have to fight me!".

By the time I got to high school, I had grown some, began lifting weights, and joined the wrestling team, where I had my first sort of formal martial art training. For the most part the bullying was no longer an issue. There were a few altercations, usually defending my hippie friends from harassment (It was the late 1960's), but I was no longer looked on as easy prey.

After high school I attended our newly opened local community college. They offered some non-credit evening classes including yoga and karate. I began studying yoga with a woman named Ann Hechler who taught me a lot about relaxation, breath control, flexibility, and most importantly, meditation. I continued studying with her for a few years, eventually helping her teach the beginner classes. I also started studying karate with Jerry Boyer, a young black belt instructor. While enjoying both of these arts, I began to realize that "Yoga Jan" was a calmer, nicer person than "Karate Jan". While I valued the self-defense skills, fitness training and competition of karate, I began to value the calm mind of yoga more. I felt that there had to be an approach that would combine the best of each.

After college I was focused on earning a living. I took occasional yoga classes while still thinking about finding a practice with a balance of mental calm and self-defense. I eventually found an Aikido dojo and enjoyed studying with Byron Mellinger. Aikido's methods of redirecting an attacker's energy and using one's own "Ki" or internal life force was closer to what I was looking for. Unfortunately, my work schedule started to interfere with Aikido lessons.

While chatting with my younger brother, George, a gymnastics coach, I mentioned my search for an art that fit somewhere between yoga and karate. "I think you're looking for Taiji." he said. "What's that?" I'd never heard of it. "I'm not really sure, but I've seen people doing it and I think you'd like it." My wife at that time said she had taken some Tai Chi classes in Michigan before moving to Pennsylvania and would be interested in learning more. It was time to look for instruction.

I found and purchased a video tape of Terry Dunn's short Yang form and we got started. My wife's attention soon waned, but I continued. I began to realize that I needed an actual coach to observe, correct, and answer my many questions. Luckily, Linda Rocco, a friend that owned an exercise studio contacted me. "I've got a Taiji teacher starting classes next week." I immediately signed up and started training with Rick Marth. Rick started learning Taiji while in college and later trained with E. C. Lee in Reading, Pennsylvania. Twice a week I showed up to learn the Yang long form and was also introduced to the art of Qigong. This was what I was looking for!

I studied with Rick until his engineering career started getting busy. He increasingly relied on me to assist with the instruction of beginners or to start classes until he could arrive. Within about a year he became too busy to teach and asked me to take over the classes. I kept the classes going for a few months before deciding that I needed more experience before becoming a teacher.

For the next few years my focus turned to job and family. Without regular classes to attend my practice became sporadic. By 1998 I started to feel tired and listless. I caught a bad cold followed by pneumonia. Badly swollen lymph nodes led to biopsy and a diagnosis of Hodgkin's lymphoma. CT scans revealed a mass as large as a large navel orange in the middle of my chest as well as a few other affected lymph nodes. I was soon scheduled to start chemotherapy.

During my first chemo session I went into anaphylactic shock and had to be resuscitated. Switching to a different chemo regimen resulted in damage to the blood vessels that received the infusions. When told I needed to have a port installed in my chest, I decided to discontinue the chemotherapy and take my chances. It was a deeply personal choice and not one I recommend to others.

By this time, I was so weak I could barely walk from my bed to the kitchen or bathroom without exhaustion. I had previously met two acupuncturists with a local office. I contacted them and explained my situation. They agreed to see me and asked if I would be interested in trying JMT, a modality they were developing that was somewhat based on acupuncture and qigong theory. I was willing to give it a try. Meanwhile I started practicing Qigong on my back in bed and occasionally standing next to the bed when I had the strength.

The results of my next CT scan were encouraging. The tumors were only about half the previous size and my strength was improving. I was able to start adding some Taiji practice to my daily Qigong routine little by little. I had only completed three rounds of chemo, but that combined with JMT, Qigong, and Taiji resulted in a full remission within a few months. As I recovered, I rededicated myself to Taiji practice and renewed my search for a teacher.

A few months of fruitless search eventually led to a chance meeting in a Lancaster book store. I literally bumped into someone as we both reached for a Taiji book on the martial arts shelf of the shop. I asked if he knew of any teachers in the area. He gave me the name, address and phone number of his teacher near Philadelphia. I was excited and willing to drive an hour to meet a good teacher. I contacted the gentleman and he suggested I come to his class that next Monday morning. I got up early, drove to his school and waited for folks to show up for class. The door remained locked and no one showed up. I waited for more than an hour before dejectedly leaving for home. I remembered reading somewhere that when the student was ready, the teacher would appear. Apparently, I wasn't ready.

On my way back to the Reading, PA area, I passed through

Douglassville and saw a sign by the highway; "Grand Opening – Open Door School of Kung Fu and Tai Chi". I swerved into the parking lot and entered the school. Not one but two teachers appeared! Betsy Chapman was the owner and Sara Gellhorn the chief instructor. I had found not only highly qualified instructors, but my "open door" to a larger community of Taiji enthusiasts and experts including Pat Rice and her "A Taste of China" Taijiquan organization.

For many years Pat sponsored Taiji competitions and seminars with famous masters. Since the 2012 retirement of the "A Taste of China" organization, it is no longer very easy to meet and train with such a wide variety of these experts. This has spurred me to record and share what I've learned from various teachers in the fields of martial arts, energy arts, and alternative wellness. I hope others can benefit from my experiences.

ANN HECHLER

My earliest "fitness training" consisted of rough-housing with my brothers and neighborhood kids, fighting off bullies, running around through the nearby woods, and riding my bike and skateboard. As I got a little older, I took up weight lifting and running. I joined the high school wrestling team for a few seasons and spent many hours pounding my drum set as hard as I could. For the most part all of these activities were self-directed with very little expert input.

My first real mentor was Ann Hechler, a Yoga teacher giving classes at the Reading Area Community College. Yoga was revelatory for me; exercise with relaxation. It was difficult at first learning to slowly settle into the postures, convincing my weight lifter muscles to let go, balancing hard with soft. She was also a stickler for proper physical alignment, something I had been previously unaware of and needed correction. Another revelation was the practice of Pranayama breathing techniques. These techniques are used to manipulate and improve the life force in the body's energy field, a concept I would later come across when introduced to Chinese Qigong. The biggest Yoga payoff for me was the meditation practice at the end of each session. I never before felt so relaxed and yet energized.

After continued months of advanced training with Ann, she asked me to help with the beginner classes. Following her patient guidance, while getting comfortable with her methods, I began my journey as a teacher.

Lessons received:

Relaxation with proper alignment leading to flexibility

Breath control

Awareness of Prana or life energy

Patience

Value of meditation

How to teach

JERRY BOYER

My next important teacher was also at the Reading Area Community College. Jerry Boyer was a firefighter with a black belt in Karate. The non-credit course he taught was a good introduction to self-defense. All of the attendees were new to karate. Since I was close to Jerry's size and had some wrestling experience, he often demonstrated his techniques on me. He had good control and was careful not to hurt me while showing how and where to strike or kick.

One day Mr. Boyer decided to teach a grappling technique that he said was "very hard to counter". As he demonstrated on me, I used a wrestling technique to counter it and take him to the floor. Before I knew it, he flipped me over on my back, sat on my chest and threw several quick punches to my face. Luckily for me, he pulled his punches and then helped me up. "For every counter there is another counter," he lectured calmly, pretending the exchange had been planned. "But let's go back to the original technique." He selected another partner. I realized it was not my place to show off my knowledge, thereby interfering with the teacher's lesson. He handled the situation calmly choosing not to berate me in front of the class. I apologized after class and he accepted that I learned my lesson of respect for the instructor.

As I continued studying with Mr. Boyer, light contact sparring was introduced to the class. As I progressed, he would often pair me with the biggest guys in the class. Often the contact was not so light. I was becoming a better fighter, but did not enjoy waking up with the following day's aches and pains. I was becoming mentally conflicted by the extreme differences between the aggressiveness of Karate and mellowness of Yoga and wondered if there wasn't something that combined the best of each.

Lessons:

Show respect for the teacher

Self-defense techniques

BYRON MELLINGER

Looking for a practice that was something between the extremes of Karate's hardness and Yoga's relaxation, I found an Aikido dojo run by Byron Mellinger in Sinking Spring, Pennsylvania which eventually became Aikido West Reading. I studied with him briefly in the early1990's. Mr. Mellinger was a diligent, gentle, and patient teacher with a high level of skill.

The Japanese martial art of Aikido emphasized grappling and throwing more than striking techniques. We learned to identify, blend with, and re-direct opponents' attacks rather than directly resist. We were also taught how to fall without injury and roll back up onto our feet if thrown or knocked down.

These Aikido classes were also where I was first introduced to "internal style" martial art concepts. Focusing on the "one point" energy center in the lower belly as your center of gravity and movement (the Japanese "hara" or Chinese lower "dantian"), use of the "unbendable arm" supported by internal Ki energy (Taiji's peng or ward-off energy), as well as sensitivity to, moving with, and re-directing opponents' energy. These ideas all translated well into my future Taijiquan training.

Most of the Aikido training involved partner practice with one person acting as the attacker and the other responding with a joint lock and/or throw. We would work on one technique at a time, each partner taking turns at attacking or responding.

Byron emphasized that we were there to help each other learn. While partnered with one of his senior students I had a lot of difficulty executing one of the throws. Byron came over and sent my training partner to work with someone else. "That's why he hasn't earned his black belt yet." he said. "He has the martial technique, but would rather demonstrate his superior knowledge than share it with others." He then helped me correct my movement and explained what my more experienced partner had been doing to disrupt it. He helped me to understand that classes were not competitions, but opportunities to help each other improve.

Besides barehand training, we practiced with the Japanese Jo, a short (about 4 foot) wooden staff that could be wielded with staff or sword techniques. Byron pointed out that the most of the Aikido throws used the same body coordination as sword cuts or stick strikes. He urged us to mentally extend our energy out into the weapon. He suggested that this would help us bring our energy out more fully during barehand techniques. This idea carried over into my later Chinese weapon training with sword, staff, and spear.

When the time came for rank testing, we were required to demonstrate knowledge of basic techniques. The tests also included Randori, the practice of defending against random attacks. The first level exams involved defense against varied attacks from a single opponent. I was the last to be evaluated. Mr. Mellinger announced that I was progressing well and therefore I would defend against three attackers! After several minutes they overwhelmed me and I was pinned to the floor. A requirement of this test was that I gather what was left of my energy and in a burst fling all three attackers off and stand up. This was accomplished only with the cooperation of the attackers. I realized that despite my improvement, there was still a lot to learn.

Although my work schedule did not allow me to study Aikido for more than a year or so, the lessons remained. Only later did I discover that the founder of the art was a Japanese martial artist who spent time in China during the early 20th century before returning to Japan and incorporating what he learned into his new practice. I now look at that Aikido training as my introduction to "internal" style martial arts.

Lessons:

Cooperation

Sensitivity to the energy of others

Use of "internal" energy to support movement

Awareness of one's center

RICK MARTH

O lin "Rick" Marth was my first real Tai Chi teacher. I first tried to learn from a video tape and a book borrowed from the library. Unfortunately, the book and video seemed to sometimes contradict each other. From my earlier experience with yoga and martial arts, I realized I needed a flesh and blood instructor who could give me corrections and answer questions. The search began.

In the early 1990's Tai Chi was almost unknown in the Reading, Pennsylvania area. After a year of fruitless searching, a friend with a small fitness studio told me she found a Tai Chi instructor who would be starting classes that week! I was there for the first class. This was my first Taiji experience of "When the student is ready the teacher will appear."

As a teenage fan of the 1970s TV show "Kung Fu," Rick joined an Okinawan Karate class taught by an instructor from George Dillman's local school before attending college in Atlanta. While there he studied some Tae Kwon Do before finding the Atlanta Tai Chi Association. There he first studied Ching Wu hard style before switching to Taijiquan taught by Chong H. Teh.

For his first lesson he was told "Stand like this." He copied the classic "standing post" horse stance with arms rounded into the double ward off position. The teacher then left the room. As the minutes ticked by, Rick stood with aching legs, wondering if he had been abandoned or was perhaps being tested. It was an hour later that he was rejoined and told "Come back tomorrow." These daily hour-long standing sessions continued for two weeks. His legs strengthened and he was able to relax into a comfortable structure. He was then invited to follow the instructor and was told "Now, do what I do."

The new training regimen consisted of simply observing and following his new teacher through the movements of the Yang style long form. Any questions were typically met with the all-purpose reply "Do what I do." He continued studying with Master Chong for five years until after graduation from college.

Returning to Pennsylvania after college, Rick continued studying Taiji with E.C. Lee who was living in the Reading, PA area at the time. He accompanied Mr. Lee to seminars by famous experts Bow Sim Mark and Ben Lo, as well as being introduced to Jou Tsung Hwa, the author of *The Dao of Tai-Chi Chuan: Way to Rejuvenation*, and spent time training with him at what was to become known as The Tai Chi Farm.

Master Jou's farm was becoming a gathering place for Taiji experts and students. Rick mentioned going to all-you-can-eat restaurants with small, lean Chinese practitioners and being made fun of for eating too little. These powerhouses packed away food in a way that amazed Rick, especially since he was over 6 feet tall and they were half a foot shorter and at least 50 pounds lighter. They claimed that the proper use of the dantian (lower belly) energy center during Taiji practice burned fuel. His lack of a strong appetite indicated to them his need for more dantian training.

It was 1993 when I started attending his twice weekly classes. He had recommended getting Master Jou's book, and in it I found the advice "Improve a little each day." Happily, with every session, I felt that I learned some small thing that I didn't understand before. Master Jou's book later served as a guide and inspiration during a time when no teacher was available and I was recovering from illness. In fact, Master Jou wrote that one needn't have a teacher if one would follow the principles expressed in the Taiji classics, a collection of ancient writings about the practice of the art.

Rick worked in engineering and often explained body movement and structure in terms of pulleys, cables, gears, and levers. My analytic mind found this approach very helpful; but other students seemed a bit confused. Rick would then find a different analogy to connect to those students. He also repeated some instructions over and over. "Relax your shoulders." He'd say several times each class. A few months into my training he repeated for the thousandth time "Relax your shoulders" and my arms finally settled into a new, comfortable yet strong position. "Why didn't you ever tell me that before?" I demanded as we both broke into laughter.

Rick also introduced me to Qigong, using mental intention to strengthen and move internal energy. He taught micro-cosmic circulation and how to use Qi to support physical movement and structure. This reminded me of my previous Aikido training of the "unbendable arm" which was relaxed and supported by energy rather than tight and stiff muscular effort.

I remember a time that Rick was discussing the use of Taiji for self-defense. He asked, "What is the most useful thing to have in a self-defense situation?" Students guessed things like "a weapon", "speed" or "strength". Rick suggested "How about a friend?" He continued, "Wouldn't you like a big, solid friend that is always available to back you up?" "The Earth is always there. You just need to learn how to connect with it and borrow its strength. Improving alignment and connection through one's body allows the strength of the Earth to be delivered through the hands." In old Taiji writings it is suggested that power is rooted (to the Earth) in the feet, generated by the legs, and controlled by the hips and waist to be manifested in the hands. Rick just had a different way of explaining it.

As my Taiji gradually improved, I was asked to help teach the newer students. Observation and use of Rick's methods helped refine my teaching. Rick was sometimes delayed at work and had me start class without him. Eventually his engineering work interfered with his teaching and he asked me to take over. I had some prior experience as a fitness trainer and assistant Yoga instructor, but with only a year of Taiji training, I felt somewhat unprepared to teach.

Previously he had me accompany him for public demonstrations and even had me demo on my own. He had scheduled an event at a local shopping mall before calling to tell me he couldn't make it and I should go solo. During my presentation I noticed an Asian man watching and shaking his head disapprovingly. I quickly brought my demonstration to an end. I wanted to apologize to the gentleman but he had already disappeared into the crowd. No one else seemed to notice my lack of skill as they applauded my performance. I knew I needed more training before doing any more teaching. Rick had given me a push forward.

Lessons:

Standing post training

Relaxation

Alignment

Repetition

Flexibility in Teaching Method

Dantian awareness

Reliance on the Taiji Classics

MARIE PERFECT

As I was recovering my health after cancer treatment, I re-connected with an old friend who had been training as a massage therapist. As part of her training, she learned Japanese shiatsu which affects similar points and energetic pathways as acupuncture and qigong. As she worked with the body's energetic systems, she became interested in the effects of gems, minerals, and crystals on these systems. She also began to investigate the effects of music and sound on these systems.

Although highly skilled at muscle and soft tissue massage, she found that placement of certain minerals on specific points on the energy meridians seemed to have beneficial effects. She further found that these effects could be amplified by using selected tuning forks to stimulate these points. These practices are considered by some to be bogus new-age silliness. Having experienced Marie's use of these modalities has left me with no doubt of their effects. If nothing else, they can induce a profound sense of relaxation.

I was present at a gathering at Marie's home when one of her guests pooh-poohed her practice as nonsense. He was a pretty uptight control freak who suffered from insomnia. Marie asked if he would like to experience it for himself. He confidently lay down on her massage table saying "this is silly." Marie laid a few gemstones on his body and began using her tuning forks. Within moments he began snoring so loudly that we all laughed, thinking he was trying to be funny. We soon realized that he was actually fast asleep. Marie allowed him to sleep for a while before gently waking him. In a daze he moved to a living room chair and dropped back to sleep and stayed asleep through the party. Later his girlfriend had to wake him to go home. He handed her his keys and asked her to drive. She was astounded. He never before let her drive when they were together. He apparently slept through the entire next day, but insisted it had nothing to do with Marie's work.

Marie invited Kitty Mrache from California to teach classes on Universal White Time Gemstone and Mineral Healing in Reading, Pennsylvania. I attended those sessions and became a certified level III practitioner.

Kitty suggested that Marie meet and study with Randy Masters, a mathematician and musician who has taught at UC Santa Cruz, San Jose State University, and the California Institute of Psychoacoustics. From Randy she learned of the underlying frequencies of healthy bodily tissues and began experimenting with the use of tuning forks touching the body to encourage its tissues to vibrate at their healthiest frequency. Marie passed on much of this information to me and I began working with specially designed tuning forks.

Marie was gifted with the ability to sense a person's energy flow or blockages and feel which modality would work best to optimize it. Working with her helped me to improve sensitivity to my own energy flow and to that of others. This resulted in improvement of both my Qigong healing and Taiji martial practices.

Lessons:

Use of mineral and acoustic modalities to affect body energetics

Improved energetic sensitivity

CAROLYN JAFFE AND JUDY MELLOR

My first meeting with Carolyn Jaffe and Judy Mellor came about when my (then) wife was seeking treatment for carpal tunnel syndrome. She wanted to avoid surgery and decided to try acupuncture. Carolyn and Judy were working in the same building where I had been taking Taiji classes. I accompanied my wife to her appointment. As I looked on, they took her pulse and examined her tongue and overall appearance. After a quick consultation they had a plan of treatment. As they got ready Dr. Jaffe asked if I liked my current logistics job (I didn't) and would I like to learn acupuncture. Surprised, I mumbled something about not having time to go back to school. Carolyn replied that she and Judy were qualified to teach and I could work with them in my spare time, practicing under their guidance. My wife quickly vetoed the idea of me sticking any needles in her. They treated her and we left with a reminder to consider their offer of training.

The next morning my wife woke up and happily announced that her wrists didn't hurt at all anymore. Acupuncture became her first choice for treatment of any ailments. Meanwhile, I changed from one stressful job to another, having forgotten about the offer to learn acupuncture. My Taiji mentor was no longer teaching,

I was working much more than 40 hours a week, and my energy levels seemed to be dropping.

After a year of declining energy, multiple colds, bouts of bronchitis, pneumonia, and asthma, I was finally diagnosed with Hodgkin's lymphoma. A CT scan revealed a mass the size of a softball in my chest as well as a few other enlarged lymph nodes. By then I could barely walk a few steps without exhaustion. I was soon started on a six-course plan of chemotherapy.

My first treatment resulted in my being resuscitated after going into anaphylactic shock from an extreme reaction to bleomycin. (I should mention that this type of reaction occurs in very few patients.) Treatments later resumed with a different set of drugs. Having my hair fall out and experiencing minor nausea were expected and endurable. Unfortunately, I was also unusually sensitive to the nitrogen mustard infusion that damaged my veins, swelling my arms and making it difficult to receive further infusions. The doctors suggested having a port installed in my chest. Following a few days of soul searching I officially informed the oncologist of my decision to discontinue chemo. I had read about illnesses being conquered by Taiji and Qigong practice and rededicated myself to these arts starting with Qigong meditation while flat on my back, hoping to work into standing and moving exercises.

My wife suggested seeing Carolyn and Judy. I told the acupuncturists that I discontinued chemo and asked if they would accept me as a patient. They were very forthcoming, saying they formerly had very little success treating cancer with acupuncture. They asked if I was willing to try a new technique that they were developing using muscle testing, energy point stimulation, breath-work, and acupuncture. I gladly signed on to be a guinea pig for this new chemical free modality.

Without going into detail about the treatment (For the curious, web search for Jaffe-Mellor Technique or SAEFET.) I can share the happy results. We were able to identify and neutralize repetitive detrimental energy patterns associated with my condition. Eight weeks later CT scan results showed the masses had shrunk by half. The following scan showed only scar tissue where cancer had been present.

Carolyn and Judy were hesitant to take credit, asking me to not tell people that they cured cancer. I did have half of the planned chemotherapy treatments, I had restarted serious Qigong practice, there is the placebo effect, and sometimes miracles do happen. I'm willing to accept "all of the above."

Follow up sessions continued with Carolyn and Judy requesting Qigong lessons in lieu of payment. They later moved their practice to the Tampa, St. Pete area of Florida and continued refining the Jaffe-Mellor Technique or JMT. I continued my recovery with a renewed determination to learn more about Taiji and Qigong.

A few years later I came across their website advertising a JMT training seminar. I emailed and was told that the seminar was being cancelled due to low response. Carolyn offered to have me visit and be trained at their clinic anytime. I told her I'd consider her offer. The next day my younger brother called to say he'd been visiting in the Tampa Bay area and was told about two women doing something called JMT and were offering seminars. He wanted to attend. The next morning, I got a call from a massage therapist friend. She had been to a body-work seminar where there was talk of two women in Florida who were teaching an amazingly effective energetic technique called JMT. She wanted to learn it. The following day Carolyn contacted me to say several folks had just signed up and their seminar was going to happen after all. I scheduled a flight and took off to Florida.

The seminar attendees included nurses, therapists, chiropractors, acupuncturists, and even veterinarians. Each of us was to take a turn introducing ourselves to the group. Carolyn interrupted my turn. "I want to introduce Jan. We were treating his wife and surprised him by offering to teach him acupuncture. He looked like he thought we were crazy and we didn't see him again for some time. What he doesn't know is that Judy and I recognized him as an undeveloped natural healer. We later heard he was ill and were glad to see him come to us for treatment. Working with him helped us develop JMT. And we're glad to have him here." At the conclusion of the weekend Carolyn and Judy took me aside and asked me to join their clinical practice. This was a little more than I was prepared for at the time. "At least promise to keep up your energy work," they requested. I was happy to accept that challenge.

Lesson:

Introduction to energy healing

BETSY SCOTT CHAPMAN AND SARA GELLHORN

By the autumn of 1998 I was slowly increasing my Taiji and Qigong self-practice as I recovered from cancer. It was time to seek out further instruction. Following a long search, I made arrangements to meet an instructor in the greater Philadelphia area. The school was about 50 miles away, but I was willing to travel. For some reason the teacher never showed up for our appointment. Disappointed I headed for home. Much closer to home I spotted a sign for a new martial arts school "The Open Door." I pulled into their parking lot and embarked on the next stage of my journey.

The owner, Betsy Chapman, and the chief instructor, Sara Gellhorn were both knowledgeable Taiji teachers. Betsy had been living and working in Europe and got her teaching credentials from Peter Warr, vice chairman of the International Wushu Federation's technical committee. Sara studied Chinese martial arts with Nick Scrima, the founder of the International Chinese Martial Arts Championship tournaments and the publisher of the Journal of Chinese Martial Arts. Sara has won national championships in both Taiji forms and pushing hands competitions.

During our first meeting I told them of my previous training. They both rolled their eyes and then asked to see a demonstration. I started doing the opening movements of the Yang long form before they stopped me and said "Oh, you had a real teacher!" They invited me into their school and also introduced me into a wider community of Taiji players from all over the world.

Learning from two teachers at the same school was an interesting and rewarding experience. Their differing approaches were complimentary rather than at odds. If there was any difficulty understanding a coach's lesson, getting a slightly different explanation from the other would often make things clearer. They were both emphasizing the same principles in different ways. I have tried to incorporate that idea into my own teaching, explaining important concepts in multiple ways so students can find their own way to understand.

Coach Betsy was the first Sun style Taiji expert I ever met. She learned the style first from Peter Warr in Britain and later had the chance to travel to China to study with Madam Sun Jianyun, daughter and main inheritor of the style's founder, Sun Lutang. Practicing Sun style's active stepping improved my agility and eventually helped me to be comfortable with the stepping in the Yang style's lesser-known fast fighting form.

For years Betsy tried to get me to enter competitions. She was a well-respected tournament judge and believed that preparing for competition increased the urgency to hone one's skills. I did agree to compete in the 2005 USWU northeast regional tournament in Hershey, Pennsylvania, earning my first gold medal. "Congratulations, you've qualified for the Nationals in Las Vegas!" she said, "You'd better start training harder." During the next weeks Coach Betsy drilled me on how to enter the competition ring, properly salute the judges and refine my movements. In August 2005 I was awarded the USWU national gold medal for Yang style Taijiquan. As Coach Chapman hung the medal around my neck she whispered "It's about time." and smiled. I didn't realize it at the time, but having that national championship on my resume later enabled me to launch a successful teaching career.

Coach Sara had a very direct approach to teaching. At first, my Yang style postures were somewhat condensed. Sara asked me to open them up. I expanded a little. Firmly she said "Bigger." I opened a little more. Frustrated she ordered "Make it stupidly big!" I opened into what I thought was an exaggerated posture. "That's more like it." She explained that my attempt to be relaxed in the postures was keeping my joints from opening. She helped me to understand the difference between relaxing into an undesirable collapsed state and attaining the more desirable expanded relaxation that allowed space in the joints known in Taiji as "song." The Mandarin word "song" is usually wrongly translated as relaxation but is more accurately understood as releasing excess muscular tension to open up. It is important in achieving "Peng" energy, an essential characteristic springiness in the body of a skillful Taiji practitioner.

She also greatly helped my understanding of push hands skills and fajin, or explosive power. Two-person pushing saras training improves sensitivity to your own structure and the structure of others, especially as it applies to exerting force and neutralizing force applied to you by others. Being able to feel the speed and direction of force being applied by an opponent allows one to protect their own center by moving slightly and applying slight force to redirect the incoming power. This sensitivity also allows one to feel where to apply force to weakness in an opponent's structure. This should be learned from an experienced teacher.

Fajin refers to the explosive release of stored energy to strike, kick, or push. It should also be learned gradually from an experienced teacher. When performed it is important to exhale and relax while letting the energy out. Sara shared that most people will wrongly cut off their exhale at the end of the movement thus cutting off the energy. She had me practice having a slight exhale follow through along with physical relaxation to fully send out the energy of the technique. Developing push hands and fajin skills are essential steps to move one's Taiji practice from exercise system into an effective martial art.

I've spent many years as a student of Betsy and Sara, but the biggest gifts they bestowed were not technical, but rather their friendship, encouragement, and the occasional push to expand my horizons through teaching, competition, and studying with others. They selected me to be their first Black Sash candidate in Internal Style Martial Arts, awarding instructor status. They required me to study Taiji history and theory, reading "The Taiji Classics," a collection of ancient writings by masters of the art. They were able to bring in well-known Taiji masters for seminars at their school and urged me to attend events presented by Pat Rice's "A Taste of China" organization. They also made sure I knew the proper etiquette for greeting and gifting respected teachers. For all their teaching and continued friendship, I thank them deeply.

Lessons:

Reinforcement of Taiji and Qigong basic principles and theory

Addition of agility, sensitivity, and fajin training

Use of multiple teaching approaches

Expansion of horizons

Situational etiquette

Awareness of the larger Taiji family

JOSE JOHNSON

One of the first guest instructors I met at Coach Betsy Chapman's school was Jose Johnson. Jose was a top student of Nick Gracenin, and a five-time national Taiji champion. He was also a member of the U.S. team that competed at the world championships in Fuzhou China. My coaches Betsy and Sara were regularly travelling to his school near Harrisburg Pennsylvania to take advanced lessons with him. At their invitation he visited and gave a Taiji seminar. Although I don't remember exactly what he taught that day, I remember that he was very down to earth and friendly. We chatted and discovered that both of us had spent time as professional musicians. We connected through that shared experience as well as through our love of Taiji.

Over the years our paths have crossed many times; in fact, we shared more than a few meals and drinks together. He often assisted Nick Gracenin when teaching martial applications or Taiji weapons. I remember working with a partner on a qinna wrist lock during a seminar. Jose came over and explained how to use a slight spiraling action to make the lock easier to apply and more effective. I have since studied chan si jin "silk reeling" exercises with Jose and a few other teachers learning to apply this spiral energy to other martial applications. Eventually I began to understand how to also use this action to neutralize the attacks of others.

I've met many Taiji players that are lacking this silk reeling skill.

Many even wrongly insist that it is part of only Chen style and not in Yang or other styles at all. Although not obvious in many modern beginner practices, it is an important though subtle necessity for effective Taiji martial ability and health promotion.

Jose became a successful workshop presenter and graduated from assisting at seminars to becoming part of the regular "A Taste of China" teaching faculty. In 2009 both he and I were recruited to act as venue managers during the "International Tai Chi Chuan Symposium on Health, Education, and Cultural Exchange" at Vanderbilt University in Nashville, Tennessee. Five hundred Taiji enthusiasts from around the world attended a week of training with the grandmasters of the five main family styles of Taijiquan.

The attendees were divided into two large groups as the training areas were not large enough to accommodate everyone at once. Jose and Sara Gellhorn hosted at one venue while Julie Nieznay and I managed the other. Everyone had the opportunity to take workshops with Grandmasters Yang Zhenduo, Chen Zhenglei, Ma Hailong, Sun Yongtian, and Wu Wenhan. Jose and I had the honor of organizing the training sessions and playing hosts to these exemplars of the art.

The climax of the symposium was the weekend showcase featuring demonstrations by the five grandmasters as well as some of their students and other well-known experts. Jose took the lead in organizing the event, bribing the Vanderbilt stage crew with a case of good beer; working with them to select music and lighting and sequencing the order of appearance. Betsy Chapman and I were put in charge of backstage operations. Jose not only organized a wonderful show, but also performed a beautiful demonstration of throwing techniques with one of his students.

Coach Johnson was always well dressed. He reminded me that Taiji tournament competition was a performance, not unlike playing in a band. Wearing a well-made silk uniform and the right footwear shows respect for the event's promoters, officials, and spectators. Ill-fitting or sloppy dress detracts from the actual performance. Remembering this, I once loaned my silk uniform to a talented gongfu competitor at a tournament.

My friend's uniform had become badly wrinkled during travel. He performed well in his wrinkled uniform during his first event of the tournament, but was disappointed by his score. His crumpled clothing looked so bad I believed it was distracting to the judges. I suggested that he wear my well-pressed silks during his second event of this national tournament. His next performance scored well enough to win a gold medal. Dressing well will not necessarily improve your scores, but dressing badly can definitely lower them.

Although he no longer runs his own school Jose continued teaching workshops, producing podcasts, writing about mindfulness practices, and playing the trumpet professionally.

Lessons:

Dress well to perform

Incorporate silk reeling into your Taiji practice

Be friendly and willing to share any expertise

NICK GRACENIN AND KATHY GRACENIN

Coach Betsy Chapman called me into her office after one of our Taiji classes. She handed me a pack of papers. It was an application to attend a workshop with Nick Gracenin in Hershey, Pennsylvania. She strongly recommended that I attend.

I had not yet met Coach Gracenin, but knew of his reputation as an excellent Taiji practitioner and teacher. Nick practiced karate as a teenager, earning a black belt before travelling to Boston to study Chinese martial arts with Master Bow Sim Mark (the mother of action movie star Donnie Yen). He was invited to join the U.S. Wushu team and won thirteen medals at six World Tournaments. He has since been elected to "Inside Kung Fu Magazine" Hall of Fame as Man of the Year and was named one of the "one hundred people who have made the most impact on martial arts in the past one hundred years."

Soon after arriving at this event, I realized that most folks in attendance were very experienced practitioners, including several high-level national tournament competitors and champions. I honestly wondered what I was doing there. I'll admit to having been quite nervous.

After some warmups Nick had us all practice our favorite Taiji forms while he observed and took notes. He evaluated our individual performances and gave each of us one thing to work on to improve our art. He surprised me by suggesting that I work on the use of my eyes. This was something I had never really thought about.

"The eyes show the mental intention," he said. "If the eyes dart about the mental focus is scattered and the movements are unclear. Look where your energy should be aimed. Work on this one thing and your Taiji will improve." I learned that vision should have some yin/yang balance. If you lack focus your movements will lack coherence while overly intense visual focus can lead to a lack of awareness of your surroundings. Some teachers recommend looking at the active or leading hand. This can lead to a detrimental contraction of one's awareness, physical structure, and energy field. Staring far into the distance is also not a good idea. Maintaining one's gentle visual focus a bit beyond your active hand allows the use of peripheral vision and increased mental awareness of both your internal and external environment.

Another piece of the Taiji puzzle was introduced during a later session focusing on the Yang style Cloud Hands movement. We started with a feet parallel Horse Stance shifting and turning right and left without stepping. Most beginners will shift in one direction, stop, then shift in the opposite direction. Coach Nick had us pay attention to our kua, or inguinal fold at the front of our hips. As we shifted right, we opened the left kua as we closed the right. Instead of stopping and reversing direction, the right hip made a small loop back and to the left, initiating a change of direction of the entire body to the left. This action was then mirrored to change back to the right. The hip action was actually tracing an infinity sign or a slight figure eight pattern allowing continuity of movement while changing direction. This requires significant relaxation and flexibility of the hip and pelvis area. Working on this concept and applying it to most Taiji changes of direction can greatly improve fluidity and stability of one's Taiji.

I've had many more opportunities to learn from Coach

Gracenin especially martial art applications of Taiji movements and use of Taiji weapons. He encouraged us to think of the weapons as extensions of our bodies. When practicing with the Taiji jian straight sword he wanted us to use our mental intention to send our internal energy out to the tip of the blade. This would make it easier to fully expand our energy even when doing bare-hand practice.

From Coach Nick I learned that there were many hidden martial applications in all the Taiji movements. He opened my eyes to a whole new way of understanding the uses of these forms. For instance, a closed fist does not always indicate a punch or strike: it can often indicate that there is a grab or qinna joint lock application hidden in the move. He taught that every move contained at least one kick, one hand strike, one joint lock, and one throw. Every step could be a kick and every kick could be a step.

He demonstrated surprising usages of common moves I practiced every day. An interesting example was his defense of a rear choke using "Brush Knee Twist Step." Shifting back; driving the shoulder into the choker's chest; elbowing into the gut; the hand striking the groin while turning to use the opposite hand to strike the face was followed by reaching back under the attacker's armpit and wrapping up and over their shoulder. The hand that struck the face could grab the head or help control the shoulder. This wind-up was followed by a powerful step forward, brush and push movement that resulted in the attacker being thrown several feet away. Inspired by that example, I have since been able to find several martial applications for each of the traditional Yang style movements.

Even though he is a little younger than me, I consider Coach Gracenin to be one of my Taiji grandfathers. Although very serious about his art, Nick has a mischievous streak. When I met him the second time, I gave him a martial arts salute as he extended his hand as if to shake mine. I reached to shake his hand and he changed to the martial salute. During our next encounter I offered my hand and he saluted. Next time I saluted and he offered his hand. It seemed I always had the wrong greeting. I mentioned this to my teachers and they laughed. "Oh, he is definitely messing with you." Next time I stopped several feet away, saluted, and then stepped forward with my hand extended. He stepped forward and gave me a hug! I felt like I had just passed some kind of test. It has certainly been an honor to be considered part of his extended Taiji family.

Lessons:

Proper use of the eyes in Taiji

Use of hips to change direction with fluidity and stability

Weapon training to improve energy expansion

Martial applications of Taiji movements

Kathy Gracenin is the wife of Nick Gracenin and an amazing person. She earned an MFA in modern dance, teaching and doing choreography until contracting Lyme disease. When I first met her, she was dealing with rheumatoid arthritis and using a wheelchair. As she regained her mobility, she used her experience to help others. One of her specialties was inner energy alignment. My teachers recommended that I book a session with her to improve my Taiji.

Kathy had me stand in an easy Taiji preparation posture; feet parallel, relaxed shoulders, head up, and joints unlocked. She observed me as I settled in. "Do you know who Mister Spock is from Star Trek?" she asked. I answered "Yes, why?" "Try growing pointy Spock ears," she suggested. As I imagined the tops of my ears growing upward, my chin tucked in slightly, the back of my neck opened a little, and the crown of my head lifted ever so slightly. The gentle upward movement of my head allowed my entire body to realign as if suspended from above. I felt the muscles in the back of my neck release and lengthen as I felt a sense of increased relaxation. Somehow, I was able to relax taller! "Good, next year you'll be national champion," she said cheerfully.

That session occurred in the summer of 2004. I had never competed. The following year, at the urging of my coaches, I entered competition for my first time, earning a gold medal at the USWU Northeast regional competition, and winning the Yang style division at the National Championships in Las Vegas. Apparently, Kathy is also a gifted psychic. I was honored when she later requested that I treat her using the Jaffe Mellor Technique energy method.

Lesson:

Pay attention to energetic and postural alignment

PETER WARR

Not long after starting my studies at Betsy Chapman's school, her Taiji teacher visited from Britain. Peter Warr started his martial arts training with Chee Soo in the 1960's. Chee Soo was involved with the British television spy show "The Avengers" where he helped choreograph fight scenes. He taught thousands of British students Lee style martial arts. Peter went on to become a disciple of Grandmaster Chen Yuhe from the famous Nanjing Academy. From 1995 to 2019 he served as vice chairman of the International Wushu Federation Technical Committee and as head judge for numerous world championships.

Our first interaction started with his words "So you're the Yang style fellow here. Let me see White Crane Spreads Wings." As I settled into my right leg he continued "Good; a little lower; a little lower yet; a little more…good." By that time my leg was shaking and I had broken a sweat as I held a lower stance than I had ever used before. After observing my performance of the Yang style long form, he showed me an optional transition variation his teacher learned from Yang Chengfu. When going from a right heel kick to the left side "strike tiger" movement, instead of placing the right foot down, he hopped backward onto his right foot before stepping left to strike the tiger. That was a different transition than I was familiar with.

When later discussing applications, I asked Peter to clarify the martial usage of "Step up and Form Seven Stars of the Dipper." He replied that there were a number of applications but one in particular came to mind. When much younger he was playing with another Taiji student after class. He used "Seven Stars" to deliver a double forearm strike sending the other student into a wall with enough force to require a trip to the hospital. He had broken his teacher's rule by practicing martial applications while unsupervised. His punishment was to receive as much pain from his teacher as he had caused to his friend. "I'll never forget that," he said.

An application he had me practice was the use of the Yang style "An". Often mistranslated into English as "Push" it is more accurate to think of it as "Press Down." Rather than shoving away, the main usage is to draw an attacker in and down to break their balance. Then you can push them away before they regain it. The "An" movement can be an effective defense to a vigorous shove to one's upper body from an opponent. Move back with their push encouraging them to over-commit. As you shift back raise the back of your wrists to bump their arms up from underneath, slightly redirecting their force upward instead of directly into you. Use your hands to control the attacker's elbows as you lead them in and down. Your opponent will usually begin to pull up and back to regain their balance. Change to shifting forward while squeezing their elbows in toward their center and up, launching them away. I've found this to be a useful push hands technique for dealing with a big push from an opponent.

Peter also helped me refine some of my other Yang style movements and encouraged me to compete. I am lucky to have him as another of my Taiji grandfathers.

Lessons:

Challenge yourself to work a little harder to progress, especially while young

Practice applications carefully – don't injure your training partners

Investigate usage – don't be misled by the names of the movements

Challenge and give encouragement to your students

NICK SCRIMA

Master Nick Scrima is the founder and promoter of the International Chinese Martial Arts Championship (ICMAC) tournaments. My coach, Sara Gellhorn, studied both external and internal style martial arts with him for several years. I first met him when he visited my coaches' school in Pennsylvania.

"I understand you are a Yang style student. Show me a martial application of the opening movement." I demonstrated a defense against an opponent grabbing my shoulders by bringing my arms up to knock the opponent's away and then controlling his elbows. "Let me show you something." He said "Grab and control both of my wrists." I did so and he threw me backwards several feet by extending his arms.

He explained that many practitioners over-emphasized the upward lifting and neglected the forward extension of the arms. Too much upward action can give an opponent a chance to uproot you, especially if one allows the shoulders to float upward. He observed that many students approach the first movement as merely something you do before you start the real moves and neglect the idea that every move has practical martial applications.

"Now, try again." I was careful not to stiffen my arms as I grasped his wrists, and was able to neutralize his forward power. He immediately changed to the down and inward portion of the movement, pulling me forward off balance. Only his turn to the side kept me from crashing into him. "The following move uses a shift and turn that allows the opponent to be led aside so he doesn't fall onto you." Then, "Okay, good, keep practicing." The lesson was over.

We have crossed paths a few times since then at his ICMAC events. He always takes a few moments to greet, chat, and take a picture together before returning to his organizing duties. His tournaments are well run and fairly judged. These competitions allow martial artists to meet, compete, and make friends with like-minded people from the U.S. and other countries, illustrating the motto "Friendship through Martial Arts."

Lessons:

All Taiji movements have martial applications

Strive to find the correct meaning and use of movements

Friendship through martial arts

DORIAN ABLE

Dorian Able was teaching Yoga at Betsy Chapman's "Open Door" school while I was studying Taiji there. I decided to work on my flexibility by attending her classes. Besides being a knowledgeable and helpful Yoga instructor, she practiced and taught Reiki, a type of Japanese energy art somewhat related to Qigong, in which a practitioner helps un-stick and move energy through the body of a client using their mental intention. After experiencing this art as a client, I decided to attend training sessions with Dorian to learn it. I believe that training helped to hone my sensitivity to the energy of others. This improved my ability to sense others intentions during Taiji push hands and sparring.

Lessons:

Yoga is good supplemental training for Taiji.

Reiki training can improve sensitivity to one's own and other's energy.

Reiki training can improve one's ability to affect energy movement in their own and other's bodies.

PAT RICE

Early in my training with teachers Betsy Chapman and Sara Gellhorn, they suggested that I attend a weekend Qigong event sponsored by an organization named "A Taste of China" (ATOC). Pat Rice was a co-founder and director of this organization dedicated to the promotion of Chinese internal style martial arts and Qigong. She was a member of the 1988 U.S. Wushu team and has been inducted into Inside Kung Fu magazine's Hall of Fame for "Outstanding Contribution to Martial Arts."

Master Rice's greatest contribution was her ability to bring together master practitioners of these arts from around the world to teach in Winchester, Virginia, helping to form an international community of experts and students. It was through her organization that I was able to meet and train with many of the best instructors in the world. From 1998 through 2012, I attended most of the July masters' seminars and tournaments that she organized. There were also Qigong retreats, classes on martial applications, pushing hands and Taiji weapons, as well as teacher training weekends.

Pat was instrumental in having me act as a venue manager/ host for the 2009 International Tai Chi Chuan Symposium at Vanderbilt University in Nashville, Tennessee. It was a great honor to meet and train with the Chinese grandmasters of the five major styles and meet hundreds of enthusiasts from around the world. She also drafted me to assist with the last few ATOC Masters'

Demonstrations, the concluding highlight of the annual summer seminars and tournament, where the teaching faculty and tournament judges would put on an amazing show for attendees and the general public.

Pat retired the "A Taste of China" organization after 30 years of success. At the time of this writing, she still runs the Shenandoah Taijiquan Center, but the end of the ATOC era has left a gap that has yet to be filled. There is no comparable gathering of wide-ranging expertise currently available. This book is my attempt to gather together some lessons from a wide variety of sources that might not be easily available otherwise.

Lessons:

Taiji practitioners are all part of a large family

Be willing to learn from other teachers and styles to enrich your knowledge and enjoyment

SHOU-YU LIANG

Grandmaster Liang began learning Qigong and martial arts from his grandfather at age six in Sichuan, China. He eventually was able to learn over one hundred routines while studying with masters of several styles. After moving to Vancouver, British Columbia he was elected coach of the Canadian National Wushu Team which finished third in 1985 at the World Wushu Invitational Competition and in 1986 was second only to China. He is the co-author of the excellent book *Qigong Empowerment*.

I was encouraged by my coaches to attend a weekend Qigong retreat hosted by Pat Rice featuring Master Liang as the presenter. At my coaches' suggestion, I gave him the gift of a small box of candy wrapped in red paper. The next morning at a group breakfast, Pat called for everyone's attention to welcome Master Liang. As we applauded, he smilingly entered the room, then stopped and glared at me. "You, I am very upset with you!" I was shocked and worried. He firmly stated "I stayed up too late last night eating candy!" He suddenly laughed and broke out into a big smile and I was able to relax. He has been very nice to me ever since.

During a brief chat I mentioned that I was learning Qigong to help in my recovery from cancer. He got very serious and told me that his daughter, Helen, was recovering from a life-threatening lymphoma. Daily Qigong practice was an important part of her recovery and he encouraged me to continue my own daily practice.

I was also able to attend his "Taiji Takedowns" seminar in Winchester, Virginia. He demonstrated many ways to use Taiji movements to throw an opponent to the floor. I began to understand that a key element of many of the takedowns was a subtle interference of the opponent's stance. Master Liang would use one hand to push his opponent's knee sideways, slightly disrupting and weakening their stance while using the other hand to push or pull them down. Another technique involved stepping into an opponent's territory in a way that would allow you to achieve a strong position while bumping the other's leg in such a way as to weaken his foundation, enabling you to more easily execute a take-down.

Over the next several years I was able to train both Qigong and Taiji with Master Liang at Pat Rice's ATOC events. During a martial applications seminar Master Liang talked about the difference between martial arts and self-defense. He stated that for self-defense a person only needs to learn one technique and then practice applying that technique against any attack. He then asked Jose Johnson to use several different attacks against him while using slight variations of one technique to throw Jose to the ground. Jose hit the floor like the coyote falling off a cliff in *Roadrunner* cartoons. Martial art, he said, involves learning a system of self-discipline, health practices and meditation in addition to multiple self-defense methods.

It was at an ATOC event that I first saw demonstrations of Liu He Ba Fa Quan, a martial art that seemed to combine elements of the three better known "internal" styles of Taijiquan, Bagua Zhang, and Xingyi Quan. The full name translates into English as "Hua Mountain, heart/mind, six harmonies, eight methods fist," often just called "water style." At that event Masters Liu Xiao Ling and Wei-lun Huang also showed their versions of the art, but I was really captivated by Master Liang's performance.

The following year I had a chance to sit and chat with Sam Masich, Ken Gehrs, and Master Liang in a hotel lobby. Sam was able to get Master Liang to tell some stories of his training and competition experiences. At some point Sam and Ken decided to play some push hands as Master Liang gave a running commentary on the techniques being applied "Ji, ji, lu, ji, an, lu, ji…" (press, press, roll-back, press, push, roll-back, press…). Master Liang eventually stopped his commentary, turned to me and said "I need to practice for tomorrow's demonstration." He then proceeded to run through his Liu He Ba Fa Quan form several times in that hotel lobby. I sat there watching him go through the moves only a few feet in front of me. A few confused hotel guests passed through the lobby witnessing a friendly push hands match and a Chinese gentleman practicing martial art movements. I was enthralled and decided I wanted to learn this "water style" art. Luckily, he started to teach it during ATOC events. Unfortunately, I was only able to experience just a taste of this sophisticated art at that time, but was determined to learn more.

I purchased a copy of his daughter Helen's instructional video, bought a copy of the ATOC video that included Master Liang's demonstration and began dissecting and then practicing the movements. In 2006 I was awarded the gold medal for "Other (non-Taiji) internal Styles" at the USWU nationals for my demonstration of the "Water Style Fist." I did realize that I had only a shallow understanding of the art but was lucky that the judges were relatively unfamiliar with it and liked my performance.

I have since had several opportunities to study Liu He Ba Fa Quan with Master Liang, his daughter Helen, and his son-in-law, Chenhan Yang in Vancouver, British Columbia. During my first visit there I arrived very early. Master Liang invited me to join him while awaiting the other students. He asked about my training and I confessed that I was using Helen's video and watching various online videos of many of his performances. Since there were variations in the performances, I tried to understand the underlying basics of each variation and work with that. He then asked me to demonstrate for him. It was a bit nerve-wracking to perform there and then in front of him. Luckily, he said he liked my version.

He explained that there were basically three ways to perform the set; "Practice the basic movements for health, or practice demonstrating martial intent, or show off for an entertaining demonstration." He encouraged me to continue practicing. "It is a Liu He Ba Fa tradition to make the art your own. That is why you will find variations."

In addition to martial art training, I also enjoyed studying Qigong with Master Liang whenever I had a chance. Qigong literally means working with Qi. Master Liang once defined Qi as energy plus information. More recently He defined it as "energy plus information plus essence." I interpret that as energy that carries information and the essence of life. While teaching a class on Microcosmic Orbit Qigong meditation he mentioned that many people thought of this as an advanced practice. Although it is an important basic practice, he emphasized that it was "only Qigong kindergarten" and there was much more to learn.

The Microcosmic Circulation exercise involves use of the mind to lead Qi energy from the lower dantian up one's spine during inhales and down the front of the body during exhales. Strong energy flow in these two major pathways supports energy flow throughout the body. This meditation is usually done seated with "reverse breathing" coordinating gentle belly and pelvic floor contractions during inhales and relaxation during exhales. The tip of the tongue touches the palate behind the upper teeth, acting as a bridge between the upper and lower jaw and completing the circuit. Rather than go into more detail I strongly recommend working with an experienced teacher to learn this practice.

During one of my visits to Vancouver we were practicing Liu He Ba Fa Quan as he watched from a couch. He gestured for me to sit by him. "How old are you?" he asked. I was in my early sixties at the time. "Your movements are very good. You don't need to learn more martial arts. At our age we need to think about what comes next." I wasn't sure where this was going. "Do you meditate?" he asked. "Not every day," I answered. He told me that he meditated one hour a day for years. "It is hard to do. Do you know what is harder? Two hours!" He explained that as he aged, he felt that he had not achieved a truly high level of understanding and began to practice more meditation. He increased his time of daily meditation until it eventually became easy. "When you reach that level, you can use your mind to travel through the universe, find the secret, and bring it back." he said. I asked, "Have you done this?" He smiled, nodded, and said, "You should study meditation with me."

The following year I travelled to Vancouver to study Qigong and meditation. I will not try here to explain what was taught. Traditionally, this should be taught orally by a master to his students. I will tell you that when mentally travelling out into the universe, one should first take very short trips so that one can easily come back. Practicing the return will keep you from getting lost when you venture farther. I have not yet found "the secret" but am doing more meditation. I have since taken an online Daoist/Buddhist Qigong course with Master Liang and his daughter, Helen.

It is important to understand that not every kind of Qigong is good for you. Much martial Qigong is effective at improving short term survivability in battle, but damages long-term health. In general, health promoting Qigong should be relatively gentle and comfortable. Avoid straining to "pack" energy. There are practices that build resistance to pain from opponents' strikes. In *Qigong Empowerment* there is a picture of Shou-Yu striking himself on the forehead with a baseball bat. When I asked him about that practice he said "That is for stupid young men," It was included in his comprehensive overview of Qigong techniques, but recommends against it as a health practice.

Master Liang once told a story about witnessing a demonstration of Ling Kong Jing or "empty force." During a visit back to China he was able to attend a performance by a well-known master of Qigong and martial art in a theater. He could tell by watching that this person was highly skilled. The presentation ended with a demonstration of Ling Kong Jing. The master was able to throw attackers aside without touching them. When the performance was over Master Liang went backstage to meet and congratulate this master, but was also eager to ask him about the "empty force" he exhibited. He wanted to feel this force himself. The Chinese master explained that he knew of Master Liang by reputation (Liang Shou-Yu being a famous name in Chinese martial arts) and was too tired to give him a good demonstration. "Please come to my hotel tomorrow and I will let you feel this force after I have rested." Master Liang woke up early the next morning and visited the hotel. He decided to wait in the lobby and asked the clerk to tell him when the guest arose. The clerk then explained "He packed up and left last night."

Although disappointed by the disappearance, he thought the demonstration was real, but showed not the ability to knock away determined attackers but the sensitivity of the student attackers to their teacher's energy. While believing Ling Kong Jing to be possible, he hadn't been able to find anyone able to let him feel it.

Belief can be a good thing if balanced by a little healthy skepticism. If a Taiji or Qigong teaching seems strange, it is better to research the information a little further rather than accepting it as gospel. Master Liang once made a recommendation to drink a big glass of water upon waking. A seminar attendee asked "Hot or cold?" "Cold," he replied. I later learned that this person thought the water should be "ice cold" when he only meant to not heat it as for tea. This is one way that incorrect information can propagate. It is better to ask and research before adopting a new practice.

Lessons:

A small gift can help make a personal connection.

Importance of a strong foundation

Understanding the difference between self-defense and martial art

Study the basics well, then make the art your own

Reverse breathing

Importance of meditation

Differentiate between martial and health Qigong

Balance belief with skepticism

Research before adopting a strange new practice

Qi = energy + information + essence

FELIX CHANG

The first "A Taste of China" organization's weekend Qigong retreat I attended allowed me to meet Dr. Felix Chang. During a break in the Saturday session, I overheard a discussion about oncology. I was just recovering from treatment of Hodgkin's lymphoma and asked the speaker if he was an oncologist. He replied that he was a surgeon at Memorial Sloan Kettering cancer center in New York City. He grew up learning traditional Chinese medicine and later trained to be a western medical doctor. He also revealed that he was recovering from bone cancer himself.

We had a brief conversation during which I mentioned that a CT scan had revealed that one of my kidneys was atrophied with very little function. He believed that improving kidney energy was vital to my recovery and showed me how to gently pat the bottom of my foot to stimulate the "bubbling wellspring" kidney acupuncture point.

He suggested that everyone should pat the sole of each foot one hundred times each day. Two hundred if there is a health problem. "You should do nine hundred a day!" he told me firmly. Men should use the left hand to pat the right foot first before patting the left foot with the right hand. He suggested that females pat the left foot first.

Dr. Chang indicated that he could help my recovery but would only do so if I was willing to be serious and not waste his time. "If I tell you what to do, you will do?" he asked. I nodded. "You will do?" he asked more forcefully. "Yes, definitely," I replied. "I believe you. It will be extremely painful." He stated firmly. I began to wonder what I had just agreed to.

Following his instructions I stood in a long bow stance, one foot forward, the other back and slightly turned out. My index and middle fingers were curled in and covered by my thumbs. I held my hands behind my back, ring and small fingers pointing at my kidney and lower back area. He encouraged me to arch backwards while opening my chest, suggesting that I needed to open my heart center where I had previously had a large tumor. Dr. Chang encouraged me to relax and gradually bend back further. At first, he spoke quietly then more loudly until he was shouting "You must conquer yourself!" After several minutes I was able to arch back until the top of my head was almost touching the ground behind me. I realized that a crowd had gathered around although I could only see their feet. As Dr. Chang continued to shout "Conquer yourself!" I suddenly wondered if this guy was really a doctor. Slowly I came out of the backbend and did some spine loosening exercises under his direction followed by a brief meditation. He congratulated me on my efforts and told me I was a good student.

After dinner on Saturday night, he offered to share some Qigong breathing and meditation methods that might be beneficial for me. He recommended charging up the lower dantian before practicing Microcosmic or Macrocosmic Orbit methods. He warned that practicing circulation techniques before increasing the energy stores would be "Like running a dry pump, will burn up." I would study those methods with other teachers at a later time.

We started with abdominal breathing to condition the lower dantian energy center in the belly. Normal abdominal breathing allows the diaphragm to drop down to expand the lung capacity by letting the belly expand on the inhale and gently pull in during the exhale to push air out. He also had me practice reverse breathing, gently contracting the abdomen and perineum during the inhales and relaxing during the exhales. In general, normal abdominal breathing is considered to be calming while reverse breathing is energizing. It is usually recommended to practice the normal method first, adding reverse breathing under the guidance of an experienced teacher.

Dr. Chang introduced a number of Qigong breathing practices. These all relied on a gentle but firm use of mental intention to lead energy in synchrony with one's breathing and could be considered to be meditation exercises. The following methods can be done while standing or sitting. One's body should be as relaxed as possible without slumping or slouching.

Vertical breathing uses mental intention to lead energy up from the Earth through one's body and into the heavens during an inhale, drawing energy back down into the ground during the exhale. This practice allows one to be a conduit of energy exchange between the heavens and the Earth while refreshing the practitioner's energy and opening up energy pathways. This practice can be reversed, inhaling while drawing down and exhaling while leading up.

Heart centered horizontal breathing draws energy into the heart center from the front and the back. Most of us are especially aware of what is in front of us, but barely notice the half of the universe that is behind us. When leading energy into the heart, one should be especially mindful of drawing energy from behind the back, through the jia ji energy gate between the shoulder blades to balance energy from the front. Emit energy out from the heart through the back and the chest. One draws energy in during an inhale and releases energy outward during exhales.

Five gate breathing involves the drawing in of energy through the palms of the hands, soles of the feet and crown of the head. The practitioner leads energy down from above, up from below, and in from their surroundings through the five gates, and into the three main energy centers of the head, chest, and belly while inhaling. Energy is then led out through those five gates while exhaling. It is important that these gates feel open. Relax your hands, feet, scalp, face, and neck to allow optimal energy flow. If it is difficult to relax your feet while standing, try sitting on a chair with your feet flat on the floor. Don't cross your legs. The limbs should be open and relaxed. Lying on your back can allow full relaxation. What is important is the feeling that energy can easily flow in and out through the gates without getting stuck. If one senses any blockages or stagnation interfering with energy flow anywhere in the body, simply lead the energy around the obstruction. Think of the blockage as frozen energy that can be melted by the flow of warm energy around it, freeing it to join and strengthen the flow. This method is especially good for freeing the flow of energy in areas of old injuries.

Bone breathing is another method I learned from Dr. Chang. While inhaling, mentally lead energy deep into your bones. When exhaling lead energy out to the skin. This nourishes the bone marrow where blood cells develop to carry oxygen, fight infection and allow clotting. The exhale energetically nourishes the skin and hair. One can also intentionally lead energy beyond the skin to support the Wei Qi (protective guardian energy field) around your body.

Dr. Chang seemed pleased with my progress. "I'll teach you one more thing." He looked around as if to make sure that no one was eavesdropping. Quietly he said "I teach you big secret, I teach you embryonic breathing." Embryonic breathing was once a closely held secret practice. He explained that it was a relatively simple, but very powerful practice usually shared with only a master's most trusted students. His version involved simply drawing energy in to the lower belly (lower dantian) during inhales. During exhalation let the energy settle in to this reservoir as if charging a battery. Body position is seated or flat on one's back. The breathing should be relaxed and natural. The difficulty lies in mentally leading energy in equally from all directions as if from the entire surrounding universe and storing it while keeping focus in the lower dantian. After practicing the storage of energy in the lower dantian, one can begin inhaling to the belly and expanding energy out from one's center beyond one's physical body.

I was sworn to secrecy by Dr. Chang and practiced while telling no one about Embryonic Breathing for years until Dr. Yang Jwing-Ming made the practice public. Dr. Yang's approach differed from Dr. Chang's in many ways, but Dr. Chang got me started. I'll write about training with Dr. Yang at a later time.

Although I lost touch with Dr. Chang, I owe him a great debt of gratitude for his help and a big boost along the Qigong path. I can only repay him by passing on some of what I have learned.

I have included only a bare bones description of some of these practices. I encourage readers to research these methods further and seek out knowledgeable instructors. It has been said that when the student is ready, the teacher will appear.

Lessons:

Qigong breath and meditation methods

"Conquer yourself!"

DANIEL LEE

I first met Dr. Daniel Kai Lee during a "Tai Chi takedowns" seminar in Winchester, Virginia sponsored by Pat Rice's ATOC organization. The seminar presenter was Master Liang Shou-Yu, assisted by Nick Gracenin.

Master Liang led us through several movements and then explained and demonstrated how to use those movements to take down an opponent. "Now find a partner and we will practice." he said. I felt a tap on my shoulder and turned around to see a slightly older Asian man. "Hi, I'm Daniel. Let's work together." he said. "Okay, I'm Jan. Nice to meet you." I replied. We started to take turns, using the newly learned movements to gently unbalance each other under Master Liang's guidance.

"Okay, you have the idea. Keep practicing together." directed Master Liang. We continued practicing until Daniel stopped and looked around. "Why are we the only two sweating?" he wondered. "I'll get us some water."

While Daniel was gone, Nick Gracenin approached me and said "Jan, be careful with Daniel." Of course, I assumed he meant to be careful not to injure a small older man. Nick continued "He is the most dangerous man in the room. Don't anger him." That was quite a statement considering that Nick, Master Liang, and a number of experienced martial artists were in attendance.

When Daniel returned, we drank some water and went back to

practicing our takedowns. A short while later the session came to a close. Daniel turned to me and said "I want to show you something." He got out his wallet and withdrew a slightly worn card. It was a membership card for Bruce Lee's school in Los Angeles numbered 001! Apparently, Daniel was Bruce Lee's first student when he began teaching in L.A. He also proudly showed me his scrapbook of pictures of himself with Bruce.

I later learned that before studying Wing Chun and Jeet Kune Do with Bruce, he was the 1948 middleweight Golden Gloves boxing champion of China. In 1949 he moved first to Taiwan and later to the U.S. Before meeting Bruce, he studied Judo and Kempo Karate. He also was an expert in Taijiquan. In 1988 he was named *Black Belt Magazine's* "Man of the Year." Daniel told me that Bruce kept encouraging him to continue working on his Taiji because he wanted Dan to teach him "as soon as I finish this next movie and get my career established." Unfortunately, Bruce Lee died before finishing that movie.

The day after meeting Dr. Lee, I went to watch my teacher, Sara Gellhorn, compete at the "A Taste of China" Taiji tournament. As I entered the gymnasium, Daniel spotted me and gestured to join him. "Come sit with my friends." He insisted. He led me over and introduced me as "my friend" to a group of Asian gentlemen, some of whom I recognized from books and magazines as martial arts masters. Somewhat star-struck I could only salute and sit down at Dr. Lee's invitation with his group to watch the event. I am still grateful to Daniel for that introduction to these experts, many of whom I later trained with.

Years later Dr. Lee was giving a "Taste of China" seminar in Virginia. He "volunteered" me to throw punches at him while he deflected them easily. After a few punches I blurted out "You feel completely different!" He smiled and replied "I know." He explained that he had been giving Wing Chun seminars in Europe. Blocking punches every day was starting to hurt so he switched to using Taiji neutralizations.

During one of the European seminars, he invited the instructor of a local Wing Chun school to throw punches as Dan neutralized the attacks. The instructor suddenly stopped punching. "What just happened? Something changed!" he asked. "I switched from Wing Chun to Taiji," Daniel told him. The Wing Chun instructor responded. "Well, I want to learn that! Will you teach me?" Daniel told him that he would be giving a Taijiquan seminar in the U.S. As he finished telling me about that experience, Dan turned and said "and that's him!" The European Wing Chun instructor had booked a trip to the U.S. and was there with us to study Taijiquan with Dr. Lee.

Before resuming the seminar Dan mused, "It took me over fifty years of martial arts training before I was able to realize I could blend Taiji principles into Wing Chun. I guess you're never too old to learn."

Dr. Lee was more than an expert martial artist, he also worked for 30 years as an engineer at the NASA's Jet Propulsion Laboratory. He did tell me that learning Taijiquan well was more difficult than rocket science. I'll always remember him as a humble, open and friendly person.

Lessons:

Be friendly and respectful when working with others

Taiji ideas can be applied to other arts

SAM MASICH

Sam Masich is a Canadian native. An extremely talented Tai Chi practitioner, he became a disciple of Dr. Yang Jwing-Ming and also of Grandmaster Liang Shouyu.

I met Sam at "A Taste of China" event circa 1999. My teacher, Sara Gellhorn studied push hands with him before she won a national level championship, and she recommended taking a seminar with him.

He began the session by having the attendees assume a "standing post" position, arms at our side, relaxing into good posture, knees unlocked, shoulders relaxed, crown lifted etc. "Relax, relax…don't collapse," he repeated countless times. I could see a clock on the wall and began to wonder who of the 30 or so folks in that room couldn't settle into a decent posture as the minutes crawled by. My thoughts cycled through disbelief that some were taking so long to settle in, or that Sam was a bastard for making us stand still for so long, and calming myself into a meditative state, only to return to impatience. After 30 minutes I was frustrated and my back and hips started to ache. Suddenly, my fatigued hip muscles gave out and my pelvis dropped into a neutral position, my lower back relaxed open, and I settled into an extremely comfortable and stable stance. Even my face relaxed as I realized how much habitual tension I had been holding, and I suddenly understood what my teachers meant when they encouraged me to "open your mingmen" (lower back / life gate). I wanted to stay in that position, letting that feeling settle in, but Sam loudly said; "Okay! Let's do something else!"

I don't recall what exercises we did after that, trying not to let the new sense of alignment slip away. I was also embarrassed that I might have been the one everyone was waiting for. I approached Sam after the class and apologized for thinking bad thoughts (hating him) during the first half hour, and thanked him for the opportunity to experience a relaxed pelvis. I told him that I had a question. "I know what it is," he said. "Yes, it was you I was waiting for. When I saw you finally adjust, I decided that it was time to move on from the standing practice. However, you weren't the last to adjust, you were the first." He hadn't intended to have us stand for so long, but noticed that no one was settling in, and decided to have us stand longer until we started to adjust. He was about ready to give up when he noticed me drop into position. That experience led to a significant improvement for my practice. One of the best lessons I ever had.

We next met in a West Virginia weekend push hands camp. At one point he said "Talk to me later. I have a tip for you that will really help." That night there was a party in our dorm/cabin that turned into a drinking, joke telling session. Every joke got a little weirder, as the night wore on and campers started to leave for their bunks. When there were just a few folks left, I told the worst joke I knew. When the punch line landed, everyone moaned and got up to go to bed. Sam stopped me "Hold up. I want to tell you something." I thought "Oh good!" I was about to get that piece of secret push hands advice! Instead, Sam says "I've got a joke worse than that, but couldn't tell it with everyone here." He then recited an awful Canadian axe murderer joke. I never did get that push hands advice. I hope it wasn't important.

I've since attended a few Push hands seminars with Sam. He always emphasized that pushing hands was more about the proper use of the legs, hips, and the trunk rather than pushing with the hands. Unclenching the muscles of the hips, pelvis and lower trunk allows the trunk to turn and the weight to shift while maintaining a stable base. Sam often refers to this as "following the hip track." One must learn to open and close the kua, the inguinal folds at the front of the hips, to be able to shift and turn while avoiding injury and instability from twisting the knees and rolling the feet and ankles.

In addition to the physical structural requirements for pushing hands, Sam's number one rule was "Don't panic!" Staying calm and relaxed is the only way to avoid tightening up and losing stability. I have since extrapolated this idea into my own Tai Chi training theory. Don't avoid all stress, but don't let stress lead you into panic. Learn to calm yourself during gradually more stressful situations; showing up for your first class, learning the first move, gradually harder moves, push hands, applications, and even actual fighting. Learning to deal with stress calmly is a useful life skill.

Sam and I are both night owls and musicians. When we do cross paths, we tend to stay up late talking about Taiji, politics, and music. One evening after a day of "A Taste of China" events we sat in the Winchester Hampton Inn lobby with Grandmaster Liang Shouyu. As we relaxed, Sam managed to coax much of Grandmaster Liang's amazing life story from him. Training with his grandfather, competing in gymnastics, weight lifting, and wrestling; being sent to teach in a remote rural village; and evading the Red Guard during the Cultural Revolution. He studied additional martial arts while in hiding, and eventually moved to the U.S. and finally to Canada where he was offered the position of head coach of the Canadian Wushu team. All of this came out through Sam's gentle urging and questioning.

While serious about his art, Sam's teaching style is often light-hearted and sometimes a bit goofy. His information however, is well researched and examined. Dr. Yang Jwing-Ming once remarked that Taiji practice should be only 50% physical work. A serious student must also mentally ponder the principles and how to apply them. He once remarked when Sam was in attendance "Sam ponders much and very deeply, but his conclusions are not always correct," and then laughed. Sam continues to practice, ponder, and refine his art, and pass on his knowledge to his students.

In 2023 Sam published his first book, *Foundations of Traditional Taijiquan; Core Concepts & Full Curriculum,* with an in-depth examination of the five phases of the lower body and the eight energies of the upper body. His translations of the archaic language of older Taiji classics into modern English should help western students to clarify and make use of some old and difficult to understand material.

Lessons:

Postural alignment

Relaxation

Mental pondering

Humor

Friendship

Document information for future practitioners.

YANG ZHENDUO

The world's Taiji community lost one of the great proponents of the art with the passing of Grand Master Yang Zhenduo in November of 2020. He was a son of the famous Yang Cheng Fu, and was widely recognized as the leading promoter of his family's style during the late 20th and early 21st centuries. I was particularly saddened, having had the opportunity to meet and learn from him on two occasions.

My teachers, Betsy Chapman and Sara Gellhorn encouraged me to attend Grandmaster Yang's seminars, sponsored by Pat Rice's "A Taste of China" organization in Winchester, Virginia. They told me that if I wanted to study Yang style Taijiquan, "He's the Man."

The event was held during the first week of July, 2000. The evening before training started GM Yang gave a brief talk (through a translator) followed by a question-and-answer session. The question I remember most was, "What about breathing during Taiji practice?" He smiled broadly and gave a short answer. The translator spoke. "Master Yang says yes, you should breathe while practicing Taijiquan!"

After much smiling and laughter, the Master got serious. His message was to not put too much attention on synchronizing breathing with the movements, but to breathe naturally. When first learning Taijiquan, it is better to concentrate on learning the movements while breathing freely. Just be sure not to hold your breath.

He said that trying to coordinate the breathing, while learning the movements, often leads to problems with both the movements and the breathing. In general, keeping the breath free and natural allows your movements to be free and natural. For more advanced practitioners there is more to learn about Taiji breathing, but first, just learn to breathe and move freely, smoothly, and naturally.

The following week included intensive training under the guidance of Grandmaster Yang and his grandson, Yang Jun. We received detailed instruction on each movement, and held each posture for several minutes as each of the 60 participants got individualized advice and corrections. We soon learned that taking long low stances to impress the Yangs resulted in quivering muscles and drenching sweat.

During the first day of training, we were holding the "brush knee twist step" posture for several minutes, while GM Yang adjusted each student. While holding that posture I was suddenly pushed from behind. As I struggled to regain my balance I was pushed again. While turning to look back I heard the translator say "He wants you to lean forward a little." and I saw a grinning Yang Zhenduo nodding and indicating a slightly forward slant of the upper body. I had previously focused on keeping a strictly vertical position. After adjustment, I realized that was, in fact, a weak position for applying power. Meeting resistance with the arms connected to your strictly upright torso while powering forward with the legs can result in your upper body being bent backwards, losing power and risking injury. A slight forward lean while maintaining a lifted crown, lengthened neck, and a dropped tailbone/sacrum opened the lower back (mingmen), resulting in optimum connection of power from the back foot to the extended hand without sacrificing balance. I, of course, thanked him for the correction.

On the morning of the second training day, I woke up with my legs so sore I could barely walk! I considered giving up and going home. After a long, hot shower, I dragged myself to the training hall only to find many other attendees struggling to ascend the steps to the entrance. It helped to know I was not alone in my pain. Thankfully, the pain eased as we warmed up and continued our practice. By the end of the week, I was not only pain free, but my low stances were lower than ever and holding a posture for several minutes was no longer difficult.

Another concept Grandmaster Yang emphasized was the outward expansion of energy from the center of the body to the periphery. For instance, he would bring his left arm up into the "ward-off" position and use his right hand to pat his left shoulder, then elbow, and then wrist, saying "Kao, jou, peng," meaning shoulder, elbow, whole arm and body. He repeated this process for most of the movements of the long form until "Kao, jou, peng" was etched into our brains.

Four important lessons were reinforced that week: First, breathe naturally; don't be overly concerned with syncing movement and breathing. Second, a slight forward lean in alignment with force application can help stabilize your structure. Third, during Taiji movements, the energy expands out from the center to support the body's entire structure. Fourth, working hard, without giving up, can result in noticeable improvement in a relatively short time.

The last time I saw Grandmaster Yang was at the 2009 International Tai Chi Symposium at Vanderbilt University in Nashville, Tennessee. It was attended by approximately 500 people from around the globe. I was venue manager and host for the large gymnasium where much of the week-long Taiji form training was held. Yang Zhenduo taught the Yang 13 Essentials form to groups of 250 students. He displayed an upright, almost royal bearing, belying his 83 years. His movements were precise and his voice was so strong it almost blew up the sound system. It was inspiring to see how the practice of Taijiquan could help one stay healthy and vital into senior citizenship.

I was honored to be allowed to host GM Yang and to help lead the group Yang Style practice from the front of the room. I still treasure the signed certificate of appreciation received at the end of the symposium.

Grandmaster Yang Zhenduo will be greatly missed and long remembered for his openness, humor, and contributions to the Taiji community and the world.

Lessons:

Functional structure

Relaxed, natural breath

Energy expands out from the center

Hard work produces results

YANG JUN

Yang Jun is the grandson and protégé of the late Grandmaster Yang Zhenduo and the great-grandson of the famous Yang Cheng Fu. He is widely recognized as the lineage holder of the Yang family Taijiquan system. From age five through early adulthood he trained under the watchful eye of his grandfather. In 1989 he graduated from Shanxi University with a degree in physical education and began travelling with his grandfather to help him teach.

I first met Yang Jun in the summer of 2000 when he assisted his grandfather, Grandmaster Yang Zhenduo, at a week-long training in Winchester, Virginia. GM Yang gave verbal instruction through a translator, while his grandson demonstrated the postures, often holding them for several minutes while his grandfather pointed out details of proper form. Yang Jun's movements and postures were precise and steady. He had an impressive ability to hold difficult positions for a long time without much difficulty.

I was able to study with Yang Jun a few times after that in seminars at Andy Lee's school in New Jersey and at Pat Rice's in Winchester, Virginia. During one of these seminars, we were working on "single whip." As I stood in that posture Master Yang approached and made a slight correction. Although my eyes were looking straight ahead past my forward hand, I had not fully turned my head that way. He gently turned my head and said, "When you look in that direction, point your nose in that direction. Don't just look out the corner of your eye." My neck had been injured in a car accident and I had developed the habit of not turning my head enough. Correcting that mistake helped me regain better mobility of my neck. I also realized that there was improved peripheral vision when my eyes and nose faced the same direction.

Another correction I received from Yang Jun involved use of the "empty" stance. Early on I was under the impression that almost one hundred percent of one's weight was held by the rear leg when performing "White Crane" with the front foot toes lightly touching the floor, or the front heel touching while practicing "Fist Under Elbow." Master Yang instructed me to put a little more pressure on my front foot during any "empty stance" posture. He had me sit my hips back slightly to balance a slight forward lean of the upper body while putting a little pressure on the front foot. This was to be carried over into all "empty" stances.

In one of the seminars, he had us practice "part horse's mane" repeatedly. We shifted back and forth in a bow stance, gathering in and opening up over and over while gradually increasing our speed. I counted over eighty repetitions starting very slowly and working our way up to explosive power and speed. Many participants were somewhat surprised by this type of training, having only practiced the more common slow-motion training. He mentioned that moving slowly is done to improve balance, structure, focus, and co-ordination, so that we can eventually learn to move quickly while maintaining those qualities. He reminded us that Taijiquan is a martial art. Only by learning to do the moves quickly will one ever be able to use it effectively as self-defense.

In 2009 Grandmaster Yang Zhenduo named Yang Jun as the official inheritor of the Yang family Taijiquan system. Yang Jun and his family now live in Washington state, USA. He speaks English well and can both demonstrate and explain concepts very well. Master Yang continues to travel and teach throughout the world, carrying on his family's tradition.

Lessons:

Turn your head to the direction you are looking.

Keep some pressure on front foot during empty stances.

Yang Taijiquan has still, slow, and fast practices.

YANG JWING-MING

Dr. Yang Jwing-Ming is the author of many excellent books on Taijiquan, Qigong, and the White Crane style martial art. Although his family name is Yang, he is not directly related to the family of Yang Luchan and Yang Chengfu of Yang style Taijiquan fame. He does, however practice and teach a version of the Yang family art.

Born in Taiwan, he began his studies of White Crane gongfu as a teenager. He was encouraged to also study Taijiquan to help heal painful stomach ulcers. He continued martial art studies while attending college and serving in the Taiwanese air force. He earned his MS degree in physics from the National Taiwan University before coming to the U.S. to study mechanical engineering at Perdue University, earning his PhD in 1978. In 1984 Dr. Yang "Jumped out of the Matrix." (in his own words) leaving his engineering career to research and teach Chinese martial and energy arts. He founded YMAA martial arts schools and YMAA Publication Center to pass on what he has learned.

Dr. Yang was a popular presenter at Pat Rice's ATOC summer seminars and autumn Qigong retreats which gave me many opportunities to study and interact with him. He told me that he owed a debt to Pat Rice for inviting him to her events when he was still relatively unknown. He said he was also indebted to Jou Tsung Hwa. Apparently, many of the older generation experts didn't know him and wondered if he should be teaching and publishing books on Taiji. During an ATOC event Master Jou came to his hotel room and began asking questions to test his knowledge of the Taiji classics and Taiji theory. Once satisfied he led Dr. Yang to another hotel room where a group of older teachers were gathered. Master Jou had Dr. Yang repeat all his answers for the group and then announced "He should be recognized as a master!" He was then welcomed to the group. Dr. Yang considered that a major event in his life and career.

I first met Dr. Yang at an ATOC Taijiquan tournament circa 2000. Dr. Daniel Lee, who had befriended me during an earlier Taiji seminar, introduced me to a group of Chinese gentlemen that were watching the competition. I recognized Dr. Yang as the author of some books I'd read and was slightly star-struck. We next met at an ATOC Qigong retreat featuring his teaching. When he arrived from the airport Pat Rice asked me to help him move boxes of his books and videos related to the weekend's practices. He seemed to remember me from our previous meeting and thanked me for my assistance.

Like most ATOC retreats there was a Friday night introduction followed by Saturday morning and afternoon training sessions. After dinner on Saturday night there was a friendly gathering with attendees taking turns providing entertainment for the group. Some sang or told stories or jokes. Some performed martial arts demonstrations. Someone introduced a game that was a cross between tug-of-war and pushing hands. Players stood about ten feet apart on round discs approximately one foot in diameter holding a length of rope between them. Players would try to get their opponents to step off their disc or let go of the rope to win. Whoever won would play against another challenger. After a few rounds, Pat Rice suggested that I be the final challenger. I managed to win my match and be declared champion. I thought that was the end of the playful competition. Instead, Pat invited Dr. Yang to play against me!

I settled in determined not to embarrass myself by losing immediately. The game began as I concentrated on not being pulled off balance. The contest seemed to last a long time, neither of us losing our balance. I gave rope as he pulled and gathered rope in when I could. Suddenly there was no resistance and I realized I had captured the rope. My victory quickly turned sour as it dawned on me that Dr. Yang should have won. I quickly saluted him and thanked him for letting me win. I still don't know if I won or he allowed me to win, but he always had a friendly greeting for me whenever we saw each other although he always called me "Yahn," the European pronunciation of my name. (My parents called me Jan as in the English pronunciation of the month January.)

Over the years, training with Dr. Yang varied from classroom lectures to experiential two person pushing hands. He brought his scientific background of research and experimentation into his examination of traditional martial and energetic arts, and into his practice. Many times, he mentioned that Taiji training was only fifty percent physical practice and fifty percent mental "pondering." He would often remind students that he was only expressing his theories, and that everyone should ponder and experiment before deciding for themselves whether his ideas were valid.

Memorable moments with Dr. Yang include an ATOC seminar he taught based on tracing the curves of the Taiji yin/yang diagram. Emphasis was on using one's whole body, shifting weight and turning, to move the arms and hands along the arcing paths of the diagram. The first part of the class involved individual practice of the yang portion of the Taiji symbol, followed by partner practice. Partners would gently connect one hand or wrist to their partner's. One player would trace the diagram while the other would move in a way that kept the connection. Luckily, I was able to work with my partner Julie Nieznay and long-time coaches Betsy Chapman and Sara Gellhorn. We were used to working together and the exercises went smoothly. Some of the other attendees were struggling a bit, so Dr. Yang split us up to partner with others and that went pretty smoothly. Next, he introduced the yin side pattern. He told us that the yin pattern was usually only taught to a master's most trusted long-time students. Any of the older masters kept some secret techniques in case they would have to defend themselves from a rebellious student. After we ineptly struggled to perform this exercise for several minutes, I heard him softly say "Maybe that's not why they don't teach this to everyone." He then told us to keep practicing, excused himself and left the room for several minutes. We learned afterward that he complained that we were so bad at the second exercise that we gave him a headache.

Another lesson from Dr. Yang involved grabbing and clinging. He lectured "If an opponent grabs your wrist, don't panic and think he's got you. Instead realize that you've got them." According to Dr. Yang grabbing and clinging tightly interferes with one's sensitivity to the opponent and allows the opponent to feel your intention. Being gripped tightly by an opponent can allow you to feel their intention, neutralize and take advantage of their tension. Someone asked "What if they grasp you with both hands?" "Now you've really got them! You know where both of their hands are and they're even easier to control. It is most important that you don't panic, but realize that they have given you an advantage."

Dr. Yang was very interested in reconciling ancient teachings with modern science. Having a unique approach to Qigong, he theorized that the vital Qi energy in the human body might actually be bioelectricity, and could be manipulated through meditation and exercise. Various tissues of the body could act as conductors, insulators, and capacitors. Even human bone has been shown to have piezoelectric properties. Piezoelectric materials produce electrical charges when physically stressed. He reasoned that Taiji and Qigong movements could gently stress the skeletal bones causing their piezoelectric makeup to produce small electrical output. According to Dr. Yang, the human brain could provide the electromotive force to move the Qi energy, and the acupuncture meridians might act as conductors. He theorized that keeping one's muscles somewhat relaxed during Taiji and Qigong practice might lower the electrical resistance to the energy flow, allowing stronger Qi flow to energize the movements. This could be an interesting topic for future scientific research.

Dr. Yang has often mentioned his goal of using Qigong meditation to "open the third eye" and reach spiritual enlightenment. He proposed dropping our societal masks and becoming honest to reach that goal. He showed his own honesty when he revealed during a Qigong lecture that his drive to research, teach and do good in the world was driven by a desire to make up for stealing food when he was a child.

In another lecture Dr. Yang used a strange analogy, comparing the difficulty of understanding Qigong and its effects to accepting the idea of "UFOs visiting from other dimensions." "What?" I thought to myself, "Did he say UFOs from other dimensions?" No one else seemed to notice that strange comment. Dr. Yang looked at me and noticed my confusion. "It's true." he said, and explained that while serving in the military, he was present in an air force control tower in Taiwan. Unusual blips showed up on the radar screen. Fighter jets were scrambled to the area and reported seeing flying saucers. When the pilots got closer, the UFOs would disappear both from the pilot's sight and the tower radar screen only to reappear at a different location. Dr. Yang's logical assumption was that these vehicles did not fly in from another location but jumped in and out from another dimension. Leaving me to digest that, he returned to his Qigong lecture.

Another memory of Dr. Yang also occurred during a Qigong lecture. He was discussing the wide variety of little known or secret practices, and among them mentioned "Embryonic Breathing." I immediately perked up because I hadn't heard that term since that practice was introduced to me by Dr. Felix Chang a few years before. Dr. Yang noticed my interest and quickly said "Oh Jan, you're not ready for that yet." I didn't tell him that I had already been practicing it for a few years. When I saw him again the following year, he greeted me and said "Jan, I have something for you. Only thirty dollars, it's my new book on Embryonic Breathing. Some ask why thirty dollars for a paperback book. It took me thirty years of research. That's only one dollar per year!" I laughed and told him that I'd be happy to buy his book and was eager to read it.

I did read his book, all three hundred and forty-eight pages plus prefaces and appendices. Much of it was a review of basic Qigong theory and methods, followed by many translations of ancient documents that mention Embryonic Breathing. Most of these documents essentially said "Embryonic Breathing is the key to improved health, longevity, martial power, and spiritual development, and it's a big secret. It can only be orally taught by a Master to the most trusted student." Luckily, Dr. Yang believed it was time for this knowledge to be shared. On page three hundred and twenty-three the actual practice of Embryonic Breathing is introduced. I later attended a Qigong retreat with Dr. Yang where he introduced the practice to the group. He held up his book and said "If you have my book, you can skip to page 323." He looked at me and asked "You read the whole thing, didn't you?" I admitted that I did. He smiled broadly and replied "I knew I wrote it for somebody."

I did not see Dr. Yang after the 2012 retirement of the ATOC organization until December of 2018 when I was part of a small group that attended the YMAA Energy Regulation Seminar with Master Yang in Boston. It was an intensive training incorporating lecture and practice summarizing his Qigong methods from simple to the more advanced. In 2022 YMAA published Dr. Yang's book, *Qigong Grand Circulation for Spiritual Enlightenment* which is a very comprehensive collection of Qigong methods for improving health, longevity, martial effectiveness and spiritual development.

Over the course of more than 20 years, Dr. Yang's books, videos, and personal teaching has had a significant influence on my Taijiquan and Qigong training and development. Although he occasionally demonstrated martial techniques on me, he was careful to never cause injury. I will always appreciate his serious efforts to research and generously share knowledge of these arts, as well as his friendliness and sense of humor.

Lessons:

Dedicated research and practice can lead to achievement.

Appreciate and acknowledge those who helped you.

Use modern science to test ancient traditions.

Ponder and test teachings, don't accept blindly.

Goal of Taijiquan and Qigong practice is to become a better person.

Pass on what you have learned.

WEI LUN HUANG

I became aware of Master Wei Lun Huang when I saw him demonstrate both his version of the Liuhebafa martial art and the "fast" method of performing the first section of the Yang style Taijiquan form at an ATOC event. The following year I attended a push hands seminar he was teaching.

During the seminar he suggested that instead of trying to push our partners off balance, we should just make gentle contact and try to sense our partner's feet and their connection to the ground. I wasn't quite sure how to accomplish that, but was ready to try. My practice partner and I made light contact with our arms and tried to sense each other's feet. Nothing happened at first. After a minute or so my partner staggered a little and slightly lost her balance. We reset and tried again with the same result. Master Huang came over and said "Very good. Keep practicing."

Later that same day I attended another seminar with a different teacher. I was partnered with a big guy for some application drills. Unfortunately, my partner was not following the teacher's instructions, thus interfering with my ability to perform the drill correctly. The two of us were near the rear of the room and Master Huang and some other Chinese masters were sitting close by and observing from behind us. I could hear them speaking together in Mandarin which I could not understand. At one point Master Huang leaned close to me and whispered in English "If he doesn't follow the drill, you should take him down." I was uncomfortable with that suggestion and tried to play nice, but my partner continued to ignore the seminar instructor. Master Huang in a stage whisper said "Take him down! Take him down!" Although I risked disappointing Master Huang, I instead followed Coach Gellhorn's earlier suggestion "If you are paired with an uncooperative partner, excuse yourself, go to the restroom and hope they find another partner by the time you come back." The ploy was successful, the big guy found another partner. Unfortunately, I could tell that Wei Lun was disappointed in my failure to teach my partner a lesson.

Wei Lun Huang was a serious and dedicated practitioner and teacher of internal style martial arts capable of lightning-like speed and extremely low stances. I confess that I had somehow forgotten his instruction to sense an opponent's feet during push hands and applications. Writing this has reminded me to start working on that again. I hope to honor his memory by applying his advice to my practice again.

Lessons:

After slowly learning Taijiquan movements well, learn to do them quickly.

Feel opponents' connection to the ground by trying to sense their feet.

HOLLY SWEENEY

Pat Rice's ATOC organization occasionally held Taiji teachers weekend events at the Open Door School in Douglassville, Pennsylvania, owned by my teacher Betsy Chapman. One of these events featured Holly Sweeney, an experienced Yang style practitioner.

Holly earned her Master's Degree in Ergonomic and Orthopedic Biomechanics at New York University. Her presentation focused on the proper use of the shoulders during Taiji practice. Most Taiji teachers will encourage their students to relax their shoulders and avoid shrugging the shoulders up during practice. Holly emphasized that one should not only relax the muscles that might move the shoulder/arm structure into a compromised position, but one must also activate the appropriate muscles to improve the arm/ torso connection. This would both protect the shoulder from injury, and enable the strength of the lower body and torso to be transmitted to the arms for increased power.

I should mention that I was recovering from a shoulder injury at the time of Holly's visit (from a hiking accident, not Taiji!) At some point during her presentation, she asked for a volunteer to model the Yang style brush knee and push position. She turned to me and said "How about you?" She had me take a left foot forward bow stance with my right hand pushing forward. She used an anatomy diagram to point out the location of the serratus muscles (serrati) and their attachment to the rib cage and scapulae (or shoulder blades). She then pointed out that my gentle contraction of the serratus correctly pulled the lower part of my shoulder blade forward along the side of my rib cage without allowing the shoulder blade to pull away from the ribs or to shrug up. She thanked me for my help in her demonstration and the class took a break. I asked her if she picked me because she knew I had a shoulder injury. "Oh no, I apologize! I just saw you practicing earlier and noticed that you used your shoulders correctly." I had to admit that my injury forced me to use my shoulders correctly. Whenever I deviated from proper alignment, a sharp pain would let me know that my shoulder position needed adjustment.

If Taiji practice is causing joint pain, one should enlist an expert to observe one's movements for alignment flaws and adjustment suggestions. If that doesn't help, it may be time for examination by a medical professional. Don't push through serious pain. Real damage may result. During injury recovery, any increased pain may be an indication of incorrect alignment.

Holly's presentation helped me to understand how the proper mobilization of the muscles connected to the shoulder blade allowed a strong, full-body transfer of power from foot to hand. The head of the humerus (upper arm) bone should sit in the glenoid socket of the scapula to efficiently transfer power without over-stressing or injuring the surrounding tissues. To fully understand the proper use of the shoulders one should seek help from a knowledgeable instructor, kinesiotherapist, or physical therapist. In general, avoid shrugging shoulders up while practicing Taiji, but learn to mobilize your shoulder blades by properly using the associated muscles.

Lessons:

Learn to effectively use your shoulder blades and surrounding muscles.

Let pain of injuries help to teach you proper form.

LI DEYIN

Professor Li Deyin visited and taught at my teacher's school in Pennsylvania a few times. Professor Li's grandfather, Li Yulin, was a senior disciple of Sun Lutang, a famous master of Baguaquan, Xingyiquan, and founder Sun style Taijiquan, one of the five traditional family styles. These arts were passed down to his children including Professor Li's uncle, Li Tianji, known as "Flying Dragon Li." That uncle helped develop the standardized "Simplified Taijiquan" (commonly called 24 step Taiji) and "32 step Taijijian" (Taiji straight sword) routines during the 1950's. In 1956 he was made head coach of the first Chinese National Wushu Team, and has been called "The father of modern Taijiquan."

Li Deyin began his Wushu training at age eight under the tutelage of his grandfather and other family members. He later trained with the abbots at both the Shaolin Temple and Mount Wudang. He attended Renmin University in Beijing and upon graduation was hired as professor of physical education. Due partly to his efforts, Taijiquan became an accredited course at all Chinese universities.

Professor Li has been influential in establishing standardized Taijiquan routines for national and international tournaments, and has served as head judge for these competitions. He personally developed the 42-step standardized competition routine which combined essential elements of multiple traditional Taiji styles. In 1998 he organized a demonstration of 24-step Taijiquan by ten thousand performers in Tiananmen Square, Beijing, China. The professor has also been instrumental in the spread of Taiji internationally, teaching in Japan, Europe, and the United States.

During various visits to the US, I've been able to attend his classes of Taiji, Xingyi, Taijijian, and Taij Gongfu fan. Other than his ability to count to ten, he spoke very little English. His teaching was, however, extremely clear. He would show a move with precision and nod his head to indicate yes. He would then mimic common mistakes and shake his head to indicate "no," followed by a clear correction and a "yes" nod. It was almost eerie how he could so accurately communicate the difference between incorrect and correct body positions as well as the necessary adjustments needed.

One uncomfortable situation occurred at an ATOC Friendship Demonstration. I was in charge of operating the auditorium sound system and cueing music for the various presentations. Having been given a CD disc with the music for Madam and Professor Li's Taiji Gongfu Fan performance, I cued it up in readiness. They were introduced, took center stage, and nodded to me start the music. I pressed the play button. The CD player which had functioned flawlessly during previous acts displayed an error message and no music played. As the Lis stood at attention on the stage I hit play again, then tried ejecting, cleaning and reloading the disc. Another disc reading error message appeared. Professor Li's daughter rushed over, "Start the music!" While pushing the play button repeatedly, I explained that the disc wouldn't play. "Can they perform without or with other music?" I asked. "No, you must make it work!" The Lis were still standing at attention, looking towards me out of the corners of their eyes. Suddenly the disc loaded and the music began. They did a beautiful version of their fan form as I sighed with relief. Those moments of panic were worse than any nervousness experienced while competing at large Taiji tournaments.

The last time I saw Professor Li was in April of 2019. He was in the US visiting family and friends. He and his wife were nice enough to teach students and friends of Nick Gracenin's DC Tai Chi school the "Taiji San Shou Dui Lian," a two-person martial application set. Then on Saturday, April 27th, honored guests, Professor and Madam Li joined a large group for a World Tai Chi and Qigong Day gathering in downtown Washington, DC on the Mall near the Washington monument. I participated in a large group performance of ten-step Taiji and an individual demonstration of Liu He Ba Fa. There were several experts and students showing various Chinese martial arts to the appreciative assembled group. After the demonstrations we had lunch at a local Chinese restaurant.

Professor Li always seemed to be in a good mood and enjoyed passing his art to others. He was clear and patient while teaching, but very exacting. A true master of Chinese internal style martial arts, he has authored *Taijiquan,* an excellent book containing detailed instruction for performance of 24-step, 42-step, and 81-step barehand routines as well as for the 32-step and 42-step straight sword. I feel honored to have met and learned from him.

Lessons:

Clearly show the differences between correct and incorrect movements.

Work hard but have fun.

YANG YANG

Dr. Yang Yang visited my teacher's school in the autumn of 2005. He was there as the presenter as part of an ATOC teacher's weekend program. He had recently earned his doctorate in kinesiology and published his book, *Taijiquan, the Art of Nurturing, the Science of Power.*

Having been born with a congenital heart defect, Yang was not a healthy child. Living near the Chen Village in China, the birth place of Taijiquan, an uncle recommended learning the art to improve his health. At age 12 he began training, gradually improved his strength and by age 16 was able to easily pass the physical exam to enter college.

While studying and earning an engineering degree he continued his Taiji practice and won first place in the Shanghai University Martial Arts Championships in 1981, 1982, and 1983. In 1985 he moved to Beijing to earn a law degree, and to study with the famous Chen style Grandmaster Feng Zhiqiang, becoming a formal disciple in 1988. Yang later moved to the United States to study at the University of Illinois, Urbana where he earned his Doctorate.

Dr. Yang combined his knowledge of Taijiquan and kinesiology to develop what he called "Evidence Based Taiji" based on the Chen style of the art. His presentation was my first real exposure to Chen style. As the oldest historically documented style it was the basis for the evolution of Yang, Wu, Hao, and Sun style versions, as well as some less known variations. I was not prepared for how much it seemed to differ from the Yang style variations I was familiar with. I struggled at first with the differences in the moves and tempo, but gradually grew to enjoy the variations. After exposure to a few more Chen style experts, I began to see the benefits and gained some competence in the style.

While attending one of Dr. Yang's summer trainings in Scranton, Pennsylvania, I was given a helpful tip. Yang observed me performing the "cloud hands" movement. He noticed that I was emphasizing the upper hand more than the lower. "Turn your trunk and extend your lower hand a little more across your body to balance the opposite leg's stepping." I found this little reminder to be very helpful in both Chen and Yang styles. In fact, I've noticed the upper hand over-emphasis to be very common, and make a point of correcting it with my students.

Dr. Yang is not only a Taijiquan expert, but is also very knowledgeable about Qigong. While I was serving on the board of directors of the National Qigong Association, Yang was invited to be the featured presenter at our national convention in Vancouver, Washington. He gave a well-received opening speech and taught some seminars that week.

During a break between sessions Yang's sister Ying approached me. "Jan, come quick! There is trouble!" I followed her into a hallway where a self-appointed Taiji expert had his hands on Yang, trying to goad him into a "push hands" match to test his skill. "This is not the time or place," Yang demurred. While Yang was visibly uncomfortable with the situation, I could see that he was comfortably solid in his stance and the aggressor seemed to be unaware that only Yang's restraint was keeping him from being sent flying. I quickly got one of the other directors, approached and asked the aggressor to stop and leave the premises.

That fellow probably brags about that incident, not realizing how close he was to being embarrassed or injured. Although upset about the incident Dr. Yang did demonstrate one of his oft repeated ideas: Unless unavoidable, "Do not enter the fight!"

Dr. Yang is a very knowledgeable yet approachable teacher. Although serious about his art, his classes usually have an element of fun. I am honored to consider him a friend.

Lessons:

Keep awareness and energy in both arms.

Do not enter the fight.

YANG YING

Yang Ying visited my teacher's school in Pennsylvania during the autumn of 2005. She was there with her brother, Yang Yang who was teaching Taiji as part of an ATOC teacher's weekend program.

When the attendees went to a local restaurant for lunch, I stayed behind to welcome any late arrivals. Thinking that everyone had left, I was surprised to hear what sounded like quiet violin music. Searching for the source of the music I found Ying sitting in a side room playing an unusual looking bowed instrument. I apologized for interrupting, but told her the sound was beautiful.

She said she was preparing to entertain our group that evening. Ying explained that her instrument was a Chinese erhu with two strings that were bowed to produce a sound similar to a violin. She played a few notes as a demonstration and asked if I was also a musician. I replied that I had once been a professional drummer. We chatted about music for a bit before I excused myself so she could continue her practice.

That evening we had dinner and then gathered for entertainment. Each of the twenty or so in attendance took turns telling jokes or stories, demonstrating martial arts, and showing off unusual talents. Finally, Ying was introduced as the former featured soloist of the Chinese Central Song and Dance Ensemble.

She toured widely and played for several heads of state including American Presidents Nixon, Ford, and Carter. Ying was also the founder, bassist and singer of China's first all-female rock band, Cobra. We were about to be entertained by a world class virtuoso!

After playing a few pieces she asked if I would accompany her by drumming to a traditional Mongolian song, *The Horse Race.* "I'd try, but I don't have a drum with me" I said, somewhat star-struck. "I've got a drum in my office!" Coach Betsy Chapman piped up. "Just play like running horses, but watch me. There are some tricky stops and starts." Ying offered. What had I got myself into? Then we were off and running with a lively tempo. Luckily, I had played with other musicians that used subtle visual cues to signal musical changes, and I was able to follow her lead. The performance was well received by the attendees and Ying happily thanked me. Apparently, it went well enough that I was invited to join her for a few future performances, including one at the Shenandoah University's concert hall.

Ying has recorded *Blurring Boundaries, Erhu Excursions,* a collection of traditional Chinese, jazz, and her own fusion compositions including the traditional, *The Horse Race.* She has also performed on television, at the Arlington World Music Festival, and at the famed Blue Note club in New York City.

Ying was not only an exceptional musician, but also a practitioner of Qigong meditation and the use of healing sounds. She produced *Elixir, Music for Moving and Still Meditation.* I use it when teaching my Taiji and Qigong classes. My students have told me it helps them to relax and better enjoy the sessions. She has also taught seminars on the use of "The Six Healing Sounds" a thousand-year-old vocal toning Qigong meditation. At the request of many Qigong students, she has made available an instructional DVD and a "practice along" musical accompaniment CD.

I found Ying to be a very down to earth and friendly person, and I am happy to consider her a friend to myself and my dear Julie.

Lessons:

Music and sound are effective healing modalities.

Be open and friendly.

THE NATIONAL QIGONG ASSOCIATION

At some point in my Taiji Journey I had been awarded a black sash in internal style Chinese martial arts, and earned a Yang style Taiji national gold medal, but lacked a nationally recognized teaching certification. I searched for an organization that might offer that certification. The National Qigong Association (NQA) was at that time promoting both Qigong and Taiji. Since I was practicing and teaching both, I decided to apply for membership and pursue certification. After joining I became certified as a Level III Advanced Instructor and was later elected to their Board of Directors. When my three-year term was completed, I continued to serve for a few years on the certification committee.

The NQA has since deemphasized Taiji to increase their focus on Qigong. Their organization offered me an opportunity to share my Qigong knowledge with a wide audience as a seminar presenter at their yearly conferences in 2012, 2014, and 2016. I was also asked to organize and emcee the 2016 national conference's "Tao Wow" evening of entertainment and demonstrations. As part of the show, I performed Liu He Ba Fa (also known as "water style boxing") accompanied by the music of Solala Towler, who played the wooden flute.

My experience with the NQA helped expose me to a much

wider range of Qigong practices. Also, working with them opened my eyes to the difficulty, time and effort involved in keeping a large organization running smoothly. Although I have since relinquished my responsibilities there, I tip my hat to all directors, employees, and volunteers that kept and continue to keep it functioning. Importantly, my time serving on the board and certification committee allowed me to meet and make many new friends with similar interests. It's good to know they are there.

Lessons:

Running a large organization can be both difficult and worthwhile.

Developing organizational skills is important to a professional teacher.

There is value to sharing knowledge and belonging to a community.

ZHONGXIAN WU

At one of the National Qigong Association's annual confer-ences, I had the opportunity to take a seminar with Master Zhongxian Wu. A lifelong Taoist practitioner and lineage holder of multiple styles of Qigong and internal martial arts, he left his job as an aerospace engineer in China to come to the U.S. to teach Qigong. He served as Senior Instructor at the National College of Naturopathic Medicine in Portland, Oregon and was involved in a 2003 Qigong research project sponsored by the National Institute of Health. He has authored several books on Qigong and internal style martial arts.

His seminar topic was Five Element Theory in internal martial arts. During his presentation he told a story of an early experience. As a boy he was raised in a monastery where he learned martial and energy arts. At some point he thought that he was progress-ing faster than some of his classmates. Not wanting to seem brash, he humbly asked his teacher if he might be ready for some more advanced lessons. The teacher thought for a moment and replied "I can assign you an extra daily hour of advanced work." He con-tinued, "Practice your earliest basic lessons for an extra hour each day. The advanced work is studying the basic lessons more deeply."

Unsure if he had been assigned punishment for egotism, or had been prodded towards genuine advanced practice, he decided to spend the extra time and effort working on and understanding the basics more deeply. Over time he began to appreciate that his extra effort in building a stronger basic foundation of mental understanding and physical ability allowed him to better absorb further teachings. I have taken this idea to heart and have tried to pass it on to my students. In fact, I like to join beginner lessons given by other teachers so I can concentrate more deeply on the basics.

Lesson:

Practicing basics deeply is advanced training.

THE 2009 INTERNATIONAL TAI CHI SYMPOSIUM

In July of 2009 the International Yang Family Tai Chi Chuan Association sponsored the *International Tai Chi Chuan Symposium on Health, Education, and Cultural Exchange* at Vanderbilt University in Nashville, Tennessee, presenting "Traditional Tai Chi Chuan, A View Through the Lens of Science." It featured the opportunity to study with the Grandmasters of the five traditional family styles of the art. The five were Yang Zhenduo (Yang style), Chen Zhenglei (Chen style), Ma Hailong (Wu style), Wu Wenhan (Wu/Hao style), and Sun Yongtian (Sun style). For the early arrivers, there was also a class taught by Helen Wu, an expert in Chen style and Taiji fan.

The five hundred attendees were divided into two large groups for classes. I had the honor of acting as venue manager/host at the university's main gymnasium, one of two teaching locations. I, along with my partner, Julie Nieznay, was responsible for getting groups of two hundred and fifty people organized and lined up before introducing the session's Grandmaster. Every fifteen minutes of the training sessions, we would pause and rotate the front row to the back while all others would move up one row, allowing everyone a chance to be in the front row for part of the class. It actually went pretty smoothly.

During that week I was able to meet and interact with Taiji

players from around the world as well as the five grandmasters. There were academic presentations from several experts concerning the numerous health benefits of Taiji practice, shared meals, and a concluding presentation of Taiji demonstrations by the Grandmasters and other experts emceed by Nick Gracenin, and organized by Jose Johnson. Betsy Chapman, Julie Nieznay, and I scrambled backstage to prep the performers for their entrances. I should mention that the person behind the scenes keeping everything together during the whole week was Pat Rice.

During that week in Nashville, Grandmaster Yang Zhenduo named his grandson, Yang Jun, the official inheritor of the Yang family system. The whirlwind week of Taiji excitement ended with an evening banquet and dancing. The next day there was a farewell breakfast honoring the volunteer staff. We received certificates of appreciation and handshakes from the Masters.

Lessons:

Taiji, regardless of style is all one family.

Large events take a lot planning, adaptability, and effort, but can be worth it.

HELEN WU

Helen Xiao-Rong Wu came from a family of well-known Chinese health and martial arts experts. Her grandfather, Dr. Wang Zi-Ping became a Chinese national martial arts hero by defeating fighters from the foreign powers that occupied parts of China in the early 20th century. He was appointed to head the Shaolin division of the Central Martial Arts Institute, and also served at the Association of Chinese Medicine. He was a doctor of traditional Chinese medicine specializing in orthopedics and traumatology, encouraging patients to use Qigong and Taiji to speed recovery.

Helen's mother was Professor Wang Ju-Rong, the first female professor of Chinese martial arts. In 1953 she won two gold medals at the National Wushu Competition and became a founding professor at the Shanghai Physical Education College, teaching for thirty-six years and designing the Master of Martial Arts Degree Program. She continued to study many styles of martial arts including all five of the traditional Taiji styles.

Dr. Wu Cheng-De, Helen's father, as a child started training in martial arts to improve his health. As a twelve-year old in the program taught by Wang Zi-Ping, his health quickly improved. He began to study Qigong and traditional Chinese medicine. He eventually served as Director of Shanghai College of Traditional

Medicine as well as in important positions with several medical and martial arts organizations.

With this family background it is no surprise that after graduation in 1982 Helen became a teacher of sports medicine at Shanghai Teacher's University. During this time, she also studied and practiced medicine. In 1989 Helen left Shanghai and moved to Canada. Master Wu has served on the board of the Canadian Taijiquan Federation and the United Wushu Federation of Canada. She also began teaching courses at the School of Kinesiology and Health Science at York University in Toronto, Canada.

My life partner, Julie Nieznay, studied Qigong and Flying Rainbow fan with Master Wu during her visits to the U.S. and gained teaching certification from her. Helen was asked to present a seminar during the first day of the International Tai Chi Chuan Symposium at Vanderbilt University in Nashville, Tennessee. Presentations by the grandmasters of the five traditional family styles would start the following day.

Julie and I were asked to host Master Wu at the University's main gymnasium. We were responsible for getting the large group of early attendees organized and lined up. We made sure Helen was comfortable with the clip-on microphone and introduced her to begin the session. During breaks in the training, we provided her with water and a snack. When her presentation was concluded, she received a well-deserved ovation. We congratulated and thanked her before moving on to our next Symposium assignment. We didn't see her again until the end of the week, on the evening of the masters' demonstrations in the University auditorium.

The five grandmasters and other experts put on an exciting demonstration of skill, including Helen Wu's performance of Taiji fan. Julie and I were working backstage helping to organize the show. We were surprised when Helen sought us out and presented us with gifts, a small embroidered purse for Julie and a Chinese fan for me. She said that she understood that the five grandmasters were the stars of the week-long event, not her, and wanted to let us know that she appreciated our effort. That fan still occupies a place of honor in my office while I write this.

Lesson:

Be kind, it will be noticed and appreciated.

TAIJIQUAN ENTHUSIASTS ORGANIZATION

The 2009 Taijiquan Enthusiasts Festival at Kutztown University in Pennsylvania was a gathering of Taiji players from around the United States and Canada organized by C.J. Rhoads. It was there that I first met Julian Chu and was able to reconnect with Steve Higgins, both excellent teachers of the art.

I was again invited to present a seminar at their 2012 festival and was asked to organize and emcee an evening program of expert demonstrations. The festival was a great opportunity to play push hands with different folks, connect with the wider Taiji community and study with expert teachers.

Lessons:

Connect with a wider community.

Take opportunities to learn from different experts.

JULIAN CHU

In 2009 I was invited by C.J. Rhoads to teach at the Taijiquan Enthusiasts Organization's Tai Chi and Health Festival at Kutztown (PA) University. During the festival I re-connected with Steve Higgins, a Taiji instructor from Canada. We had met previously and had enjoyed playing push hands together. He immediately suggested we do some friendly pushing together. We played for a while and then took a break.

A young (20ish) Asian man approached and asked if he could play. "My teacher said I should push with you." I agreed and we had some fun trying to unbalance each other while maintaining our own structures. I told the fellow he was pretty good. "Oh no, I'm just a beginner," he said. "You should meet my teacher." He then introduced me to his teacher, Julian Chu. Mr. Chu said that he enjoyed watching us and that perhaps I should visit his class in Washington, D.C. if I had a chance. I thanked him for the invitation. Unfortunately, I never did get a chance to visit.

A few years later we met at another gathering in Pennsylvania. I finished teaching my program and hurried to catch Julian's class, already in progress. There was a group of people around him as he moved from person to person lightly touching them with one finger causing them to stagger and struggle to maintain their balance. Each person had a look of shock and confusion on their face while Mr. Chu wore a happy grin.

"I practiced Taijiquan for 50 years before I was able to do that" he said. "My teacher, Ben Lo, kept telling me to sink my Qi. I would try to lower my stance and he would correct me, telling me not to bend my knees more, but to sink my Qi. For years I didn't understand what he meant until he one day gave me a clue that helped me change my approach. When I was able to understand and follow his suggestion there was a noticeable improvement in my Taiji skill." He then suddenly changed the subject and said "Now let's do something else." The assembled group stood with their mouths open and virtual question marks over their heads. Julian turned to face them, feigned surprise, and said, "Oh, did you want to know what he told me?"

He then explained that Ben Lo recommended that he should imagine standing in an elevator just as it begins to rise. Without holding the handrail, feel the subtle adjustment your body makes to stay balanced as the floor presses up against your feet. "Try to replicate that feeling as your feet press against the floor and your body settles. Go ahead, try it!" Julian suggested.

Most of the group looked a little confused as they tried to get that feeling. I tried to mentally recapture what that first moment of elevator lift felt like, remembering riding the lift in the local department store when I was a child. As I concentrated on recapturing that sensation, I felt my whole body adjust itself and Julian shouted excitedly "He's got it!" and hurried over to where I was standing.

"Yes, you've got it. Now, can you maintain it while doing some moves?" As soon as I started to move, I began to lose that improved feeling of stability. "No," I answered and stood still again while regaining the feeling. "That's okay." He said, reassuringly. "You found it, and now you know how to find it again. Gradually you should be able to keep it while moving and pushing hands."

Working on the maintenance of that feeling has been a worthwhile challenge ever since. The rise of an elevator seems to simulate an increase of gravity's downward force against the floor, multiplying the effect of any structural or energetic top-heaviness or instability. That increased effect makes it easier to sense any defect and work on correction. This may not work for everyone, but has helped me to improve, and I thank Julian for his advice and enthusiastic encouragement.

Lessons:

Sink the Qi practice method.

Offer students encouragement.

STEVE HIGGINS

Steve Higgins and I first met at some ATOC Taiji events in Winchester, VA. He was a Canadian Taiji instructor from Kitchener, Ontario specializing in the Yang style medium frame, which is less well known than the large frame of Yang Cheng Fu. We enjoyed each other's company and he would often seek me out to play push hands together.

As a founding member of the Taijiquan Enthusiasts Organization, Steve was in attendance at the organization's festivals where I taught. We were able to renew our friendship and play some more push hands. I attended his presentation of middle frame Yang style and followed along as he taught. During a break in the action, he approached me. "I see you know the secret stepping method." he said. I genuinely claimed ignorance. I didn't know what he was referring to. He continued, "Don't pretend. I saw you using it." This wasn't the first time that others assumed I knew more than I actually did. I occasionally did something correctly by accident that I hadn't been taught. When Steve realized that I really didn't know what he was talking about, he decided to explain.

Paraphrasing Mr. Higgins from memory, "To maintain proper balance and structure, especially during slow stepping, one cannot usually move the stepping foot from lifting point to landing point in a straight line while maintaining balance and structure." Beginners especially tend to step quickly to avoid losing their balance during a slow, controlled step. "By bringing the moving foot in near the ankle of the supporting foot before extending to its landing position allows better balance and control." For example; when stepping from a left foot forward bow stance into a right foot forward stance, the moving (right) foot draws in to a stable position near the left ankle before being placed in position for the right foot forward stance. For geometry geeks, the right foot traces a slight arc, or compound curve with the PCC (or point of compound curvature) near the inside of the left ankle.

The spleen 2 acupuncture point near the joint of the stepping foot's large toe could touch and connect to the kidney 6 point on the inside of the ankle of the opposite foot during the curved step. If necessary to maintain balance, one may pause with the points touching before stepping out. Experienced practitioners should eventually be able to use this curved stepping without the points actually touching, but merely coming close and sensing an energetic connection as the moving foot passes by. Practice slowly to reinforce balance and structure. Later one can learn to use this stepping at a faster pace, always maintaining stability.

I've heard arguments saying a straight line is the shortest distance and therefore the fastest step. It is during that fast step that one's balance and stability are briefly compromised. Compromised balance can lead to falls. In combat or push hands play an experienced practitioner can take advantage of that compromised moment, uprooting and defeating the stepping opponent. Ancient Taiji sayings suggest that one should find the straight in the curve, and the curve in the straight. They also suggest practicing slowly to learn to move quickly. Even the U.S. Navy Seals have a saying: "Slow is smooth, and smooth is fast." I suggest trying this stepping method while doing slow and controlled stepping in your Taiji practice.

Lessons:

Make Taiji friends. They probably have something valuable to share.

Practice curved stepping.

HELEN LIANG

Master Helen Liang, the daughter of Chinese Wushu Grandmaster Liang Shou-Yu, began learning martial arts from her father at age four. By age 11 she was training with the Sichuan Provincial Wushu School, and soon began winning gold medals at national competitions. In 1989 she immigrated to Canada and joined her father's school as an instructor.

Helen studied economics at the University of British Columbia. She graduated and got a job at a Vancouver bank. Not long afterward she developed a long-lasting high fever. It was eventually discovered that she was suffering from an aggressive form of lymphoma. Months of unsuccessful chemotherapy led to being told that she only had a few weeks to live. She left the hospital to spend her remaining time at home with her family.

Her father encouraged her to practice meditation and Qigong outdoors for fresh air. He also found doctors willing to help with alternative medical treatments. Weeks turned to months and years as she gradually got stronger. Eventually she was able to return to martial arts practice and teaching.

She became especially well-known for her Liu He Ba Fa expertise. This is a lesser-known, sophisticated internal style martial art that contains elements of Taiji, Xingyi, and Bagua. It can be translated as "Six Harmonies / Eight Methods" but is often referred to as "Water Style Boxing". Helen has made Water Style teaching videos and can be found teaching this and other classes at the SYL Wushu Taiji Qigong Institute near Vancouver.

I was first exposed to Liu He Ba Fa in Winchester, Virginia when Liang Shou-Yu demonstrated and began teaching it at "A Taste of China" events. I continued studying it by travelling to Vancouver for some training sessions offered by Grandmaster Liang and his family. GM Liang supervised while Helen did much of the teaching assisted by her husband, Chenhan Yang.

Helen did a great job of leading us through the form choreography and explaining each individual movement. She was very approachable, friendly, and able to answer any questions we had. Most importantly for me, she served as an inspiration. Having survived a life-threating bout of lymphoma myself, it was good to see her be able to come back from illness and reach a high level of martial ability and liveliness. Helen has been named vice president of the SYL Wushu Taiji Qigong Institute.

Lessons:

Qigong and Taiji can have important health benefits.

Don't give up. Recovery from dire circumstances is possible.

CHENHAN YANG

Master Chenhan Yang, the official disciple of Chinese Wushu Grandmaster Liang Shou-Yu, began learning martial arts at a young age while growing up in Taiwan. After immigrating to Canada, he began studying with GM Liang and has earned many awards including Grand Champion at the 2007 World Cup International Martial Arts Championship in Taiwan. He has been named president of the SYL Wushu Taiji Qigong Institute, and Vice Chairman of the International Wushu Sanshou Dao Association. He is married to Master Helen Liang.

I met Chenhan while visiting the Vancouver area to learn Liu He Ba Fa "Water Style Boxing" under the direction of Liang Shou-Yu. Helen and Chenhan were assisting with the coaching. I had the chance to work one on one with Chenhan while there. When he learned that my main style was Yang Taiji, he took the time to explain how each Water Style movement was similar to and different from the Yang style movements I was familiar with. That made it much easier for me to learn the movements and progress more quickly. His understanding of the different arts made his teaching very effective and helpful to me.

Lesson:

Both broad and deep knowledge of a subject are helpful when teaching.

JOHN LEE

I first learned of Dr. Lee while trying to find a source for a better quality Taiji straight sword (jian). I had a decent sword, but after learning some basic sword routines, I had the opportunity to try some other peoples' swords. Some were noticeably better balanced and more comfortable than my first sword. It was time for a new weapon. I decided to budget up to one thousand dollars to get a really good sword.

I was told that Dr. Lee had a good supply of swords at his shop in Riverside, New Jersey. I tried to contact him by phone and email several times with no response. After months of no success, I had given up.

A Chinese Taiji student of mine made a trip to her homeland to visit family. When she returned, she showed me a very nice sword that her brother had given her as a present. The sword was so well made and balanced that it made me a little jealous. I decided to try to contact Dr. Lee again. My persistence paid off as Dr. Lee personally answered the phone. He apologized for not returning my messages and invited me to come to his shop and examine his swords. I made arrangements to meet him the following day.

My girlfriend Julie and I drove from our home in Pennsylvania to his shop in New Jersey. I was a little concerned when the door was locked and no one answered. A few minutes later Dr. Lee arrived, greeted us, and led us inside. We found ourselves in a room stacked with hundreds of cardboard boxes apparently all containing swords. It was reminiscent of the Harry Potter movie scene in the wand shop. Dr. Lee opened a box, handed me a sword, and said "try this." I tried a few basic moves in the cramped space. "The blade is too forward heavy for me." I told him. "Okay, try this one." That one didn't feel comfortable in my hand. I tried several more without finding one that felt right for me. He seemed to have made a decision and said "Let's go to the back room." He unlocked and opened a door into a room that was stacked chest high with boxes.

Dr. Lee climbed over a pile of boxes and disappeared. A hand appeared from behind the mound of boxes holding a sword. "Try this!" If the shop reminded me of the Harry Potter movie, this brought to mind the British legend of the Lady of the Lake where Arthur received the sword Excalibur. The sword felt comfortable and well balanced. I practiced with it outside behind his shop to be sure it was the right one. He also found a nice sword for Julie. "I have a few more in my martial arts school office." He offered, "I'll take you there."

There were several more swords at his school but I had already found the right one. We relaxed and chatted in his office. I asked why he had so many swords. "Around Longquan (Dragon Well) Village are many forges known for their swords." He explained. "One of the forges was owned by relatives of mine. When the uncle that ran the forge passed away, I was contacted to see if I might take it over." Dr. Lee was already living in the United States, but returned to visit relatives and discuss the forge. They wanted to keep the business in the family but insisted that he stay long enough to learn the craft and put in the work before allowing him to take over. He decided to stay and do the hard labor of working at the forge until his aunt was satisfied. He then found himself with a whole lot of swords.

While chatting in his office He explained that he had studied dentistry to make his mother happy, but eventually decided to pursue teaching martial arts as a profession. He started practicing martial arts as a young boy in China. He told us that when he was young, he once, without asking, took his grandfather's sword to a demonstration by a well-known expert. During his presentation the expert swordsman asked the young boy to demonstrate his skill. The expert recognized that John was carrying a sword that he didn't own and only an accomplished practitioner should have had. After being embarrassed by his lack of skill, he later learned how the swordsman knew he wasn't the owner of the sword.

Dr. Lee explained; "A beginner's first sword and scabbard will usually be fitted with hardware with bat symbolism. After attaining some skill, the teacher will replace the bat hardware with lion symbols. Finally, dragon hardware indicates that the practitioner has achieved expertise." I suddenly realized I had selected a sword with dragon hardware. "Oh, I didn't know that when I picked this one. Maybe I should find another." I said quickly. "No, that is the right sword for you." He responded. "You should have the dragon."

Now came the moment of truth. "How much do I owe you?" I asked bracing myself for the answer. When he answered I was surprised that it wasn't much more. He noticed my surprise and thinking the price was too high he said "That's for both swords, including Julie's." I told him that the price was too low. "No, I've taken up too much of your time. I can't ask for any more." I happily paid his price and thanked him for an enjoyable and educational visit. We then returned home with our treasures.

I met Dr. Lee again when I was inducted into the United Fellowship of Martial Arts Hall of Fame during their 2015 dinner. He was emcee and presenter at the event. When I was called up to receive my award, I reminded him that we had previously met. He smiled and said "Oh, I remember the dragon."

Lessons:

Patience and persistence may be rewarded.

Casual conversation with experts may reveal useful information.
Try to learn about Chinese culture and symbolism.

PETE VOLL

Pete Voll and I met while attending seminars at the "A Taste of China" events in Winchester, Virginia. Pete and I were both dealing with some health issues that seemed to be helped by our Taiji and Qigong practices. Having studied with Pat Rice and Nick Gracenin, he was adept at several internal martial arts, especially Yang style Taijiquan. One day he approached me with some advice.

I had been practicing Yang style and he noticed something about my form. "I see that you pull the front of your foot up into about a 45-degree angle during the postures raise hands, strum the lute, and fist under elbow. That's how it is commonly done in the modern, simplified forms. In traditional Yang style the toes are only slightly lifted keeping pressure on the bottom of the heel." After that little tip I reviewed some videos of Yang Jun and Yang Zhenduo, verifying that the front of the foot was only slightly lifted in those postures. After some pondering, I realized that the force from a heel kick or foot stomp would be most effectively delivered down the tibia through to the bottom of the heel with the front of the foot pulled back enough to be out of the way. In fact, Yang Zhenduo taught that some pressure should be put on the heel of the front foot during those stances rather than being completely empty. I have adopted this method and recommend it to my students.

Pete and his wife, Kasia opened Full Moon Tai Chi in Front Royal, Virginia before moving to Prescott, Arizona. He and I agree that teaching is a great way of not only sharing healthy practices but keeping ourselves healthy also.

Lessons:

Be willing to learn from your peers.

Health problems are not a reason to avoid exercise, but a reason to do appropriate exercises.

ZHU TIANCAI

Grandmaster Zhu Tiancai is known as one of the famous "Four Great Guardian Warriors", the 19th generation lineage holders of Chen Family Taijiquan. Having grown up in the Chen Village birthplace of Taijiquan, he learned the art from his uncles, Chen Zhao Ku and Chen Zhao Pi, eighteenth generation disciples. He has earned gold medals at district, national, and international competitions. In China he has received many honors including "Person with Outstanding International Contribution," a representative bearer of China's cultural heritage, Vice President of Henan Province Chen Style Taijiquan Association, and President of the International Tian Cai Chenjiagou Taijiquan Association. He has taught internationally, including in the United States.

In August of 2017 Coach Sara Gellhorn encouraged me to attend a push hands workshop hosted by C.P. Ong featuring Grandmaster Zhu. He led us through many exercises and partner drills before having us do some freestyle practice with partners. As the group practiced Grandmaster Zhu moved around, observing, commenting, and making some adjustments. At one point he approached and asked me to push with him.

Smiling, he raised his arms and nodded. Nervously I made contact and gently tried to prod and find his center. He kept encouraging me to push harder, still nodding and smiling. I resisted the idea of pushing harder because I couldn't find anything solid to push against. It seemed that any aggressive push by me was only going to result in my being off-balance. His interpreter then said "He wants you to push hard." I answered with a laugh. "I can tell that would end badly for me. I don't want to get sent flying!" As the translator relayed my response he laughed and lowered his arms. I stepped back, saluted and thanked Grandmaster Zhu. He returned my bow and patted me on the shoulder. "Hao" (good) he chuckled and nodded. As the workshop drew to a close, he good-naturedly agreed to pose for a picture with Coach Gellhorn, myself and two of her other students.

Lessons:

Be willing to interact with less experienced players to help them improve.

Be ready to interact with more experienced players so you may learn.

PARENTS AND SIBLINGS

I come from a somewhat active and athletic family. As kids we spent a lot of time running around in the nearby woods and fields, climbing trees, riding bikes, swimming, and playing sports. I especially enjoyed riding my skateboard and playing ping pong. I learned a lot about coaching by observing my siblings being trained by their athletic mentors.

J. MICHAEL "MIKE" GYOMBER

My older brother, Mike was my first sparring partner. Our tussles as kids helped toughen me up and he later inspired me to take up weight lifting as a teenager. He was a high school All-County and All-League football lineman playing both offensive and defensive guard. An opposing team's coach once described him as "tough as nails" in a newspaper article. He served in the U.S. Marine Corp, studied finance in college, and had a successful career in real estate. He was also a highly rated amateur tennis player. Mike has coached the Wyomissing, PA high school tennis teams to Berks County and Pennsylvania State championships.

GEORGE GYOMBER

My younger brother took up gymnastics and diving as a youngster and continued through high school. He was PA District 3 diving champion for three years. (He was runner up in his freshman year.) He competed in the PA state finals all four years of high school. George also won PA state championships in gymnastics. He has been in demand as a gymnastic and diving coach in Pennsylvania and Florida.

NANCY (GYOMBER) FUNCK

The youngest of my siblings, my sister Nancy studied tap dance before moving on to gymnastics and diving. As a youngster, she and my brother George won numerous talent competitions as an acrobatic team. She has also earned a nice collection of trophies.

CAROL (MOSSER) GYOMBER

My mother was also athletic, enjoying swimming and volleyball as an adult. She played on the Berkshire Heights adult volleyball team that won six consecutive Berks County, PA titles. She enjoyed playing tennis, practicing yoga, and ballroom dancing into her senior years. She would often ask me to teach her some Taiji moves. Mom passed away in 2023.

JULIUS "GUS" GYOMBER

My father was an enthusiastic supporter of his family's athletic activities. He attended games and competitions, driving my brother and sister to meets almost every weekend. He delighted in displaying their awards in our house's large front bay window for all to see, with our home becoming locally known as "the trophy house." He occasionally asked me when I was going to win something. I had been an undefeated junior varsity high school wrestler until I was injured during practice near the end of the season and then sat out my senior year. Unfortunately, Dad passed away from cancer before I won the Yang style gold medal at the 2005 USWU Nationals in Las Vegas. I think he'd be happy.

Lessons:

Inspiration

Support

BERKS TAI CHI ASSISTANT INSTRUCTORS

JULIE NIEZNAY

My life partner and a Taiji expert in her own right. Julie was the 2005 USWU Women's National All-Around Champion, having won gold medals in barehand and weapon forms, including her specialty, Taiji double-fans. She was also the 2009 ICMAC Women's Tai Chi Champion.

TIM MATHIAS

Tim was already a fifth-degree black belt expert in Okinawan Karate when he started studying with me. His martial art experience was very helpful in our exploration of Taiji fighting applications. His willingness to learn a new art and his friendly demeanor will be missed. RIP.

WARD LATSHAW

Ward studied Yang style with me for several years, travelling from neighboring Lancaster County, PA to Berks to practice and help to teach newer students. He and I travelled together to study with Yang Jun at Pat Rice's school in Winchester, Virginia.

NEIL DONLEY

Neil was another dedicated student who travelled from out-of-town to attend classes and assist with teaching duties. Besides Taiji, Neil is an avid Kayaker.

BEN SCHIAVONE

Ben started attending classes in 2014 and is still faithfully coming to classes at the time of this writing (2024). He has competed and won medals for Yang style at ICMAC competitions in Orlando, Florida. He has been helping to teach classes for several years.

LI-HONG LU

Dr. Lu is a physiatrist and acupuncturist that has been attending my Taiji classes at Reading Hospital's rehabilitation facility in Wyomissing, PA for several years. She is an accomplished practitioner of the modern ten step, simplified twenty-four step, and standardized forty-two step Taiji routines and helps to teach students at the rehab classes.

PAUL SEWARD

Paul has been a dedicated student and has been assisting instruction of beginners of the ten-step and twenty-four step routines during classes at the Tower Health rehab facility and at Berks Encore senior citizens facilities.

I sincerely thank them all for their friendship and assistance.

Lessons:

Accept help

Give recognition

STUDENTS

I 've had the honor of introducing hundreds of people to the arts of Taijiquan and Qigong. I am grateful to them all. They have inspired me to continue teaching and to write this book.

BRUCE HOPKINS

There is one person that deserves special mention. Bruce Hopkins attended Taiji classes at the Highlands at Wyomissing, a senior living community in Berks County, Pennsylvania. He began taking classes when he was still a young man in his nineties. Getting around without the aid of a walker or cane, he was a regular attendee at classes for years. At one hundred and three years of age, he was the most senior student I've had. He once attributed his long life to "not sitting around." Bruce is an inspiration.

PRIVATE STUDENTS

There have been a few long-time students that have taken private lessons with me over the years. I want to recognize their support and dedication.

RUSS HOMAN

Russ and I first met as musicians and soon discovered a shared interest in martial arts. Russ started Tae Kwon Do lessons at age thirteen and his interest continued into adulthood. When I started learning Taiji he suggested we work out together. He had me wearing focus pad mitts on my hands as he practiced targeting them with spinning back fist strikes. He then put on the mitts and invited me to try. I tried to remember my instructor's advice to relax the arms and use power from the legs, hips, and waist. On the first attempt my fist hit the focus pad on his hand and Russ dropped to the floor! As his eyes fluttered open, I began apologizing, thinking I missed the pad and hit an unprotected area. Looking up at me he told me that I did hit the pad and "It felt like lightning shot up my arm and exploded in my head." Then he added "I'm coming to Taiji class with you." When told about this event, my teacher, Rick Marth, asked if I had kept my arm relaxed while I used my legs, hips, and waist. "Yes," I replied. He then asked Russ if he had braced for the contact. Russ answered in the affirmative. Rick turned to Russ and said "When you braced, you gave the energy a pathway up your arm to your heart and brain. It's good you were wearing that padded mitt." Twenty years later Russ is taking private lessons with me.

PAT WOODELL

Pat was a second-degree black belt practitioner of Okinawan Karate. He got in touch with me because he had an interest in Yang style Taiji. During our first meeting he had many questions about Dim Mak pressure point fighting techniques. I disappointed him by letting him know that I had no experience in that area. He had some previous training from his Karate teacher who told him that his pressure point information originally came from Yang style Taiji masters. Pat suggested that I probably knew these techniques but was sworn to secrecy. I laughed and told him that I honestly didn't have the secrets he was searching for. Pat then asked if I would just show him a Yang style move.

I decided to demonstrate the Yang style movement "wild horse parts mane". He looked confused. "How would you use that in a fight?" he asked. "Throw a punch." I suggested. I intercepted his strike and gently followed through with a counter-attack. "I thought you didn't know pressure point fighting!" he said accusingly. "I don't. I just protected and countered." I answered truthfully. He replied "Based on my own knowledge it seems you started by draining energy down my arm by stroking the triple burner points on my forearm with your strike deflection, followed by pressing heart and lung points while controlling my wrist. You then bumped a point on the gall bladder meridian of my leg with your knee, weakening my stance." He continued. "You then used your forearm to strike the heart and pericardium points in my armpit. Done with more force, that combination can cause a fatal heart attack. Thanks for not hitting me hard." He paused. "What else don't you know about pressure point fighting?"

Pat and I then spent many Saturday afternoons practicing together. I taught him the movements of the Yang style long form and he explained the pressure point techniques that were hidden in them. An important idea emerged from these sessions. I realized that when I put pressure on his points he would often wince in pain as he tensed to protect himself. When he applied force on my targeted points, I stayed as relaxed as possible and his pressure felt like a shiatsu massage. In fact, after his pressure point attacks, I would often respond with "Thanks for the massage!" Here was a clear indication that the more relaxed muscles of Taiji were a defensive martial arts advantage. Tightened muscles seemed to make the points even more sensitive to pressure. After graduating with his engineering degree, Pat moved out of the area to pursue his career. I hope he is still practicing.

PERRY STEIF

Perry had practiced Shaolin Gongfu for some years before his IT career interfered. He decided to start training again and contacted me about Taiji lessons. We've been mostly working on Yang style for a few years and have also done some Sun style, Water style, and some Qigong. He is an enthusiastic and dedicated student.

RANDY REIFSNYDER

Randy studied other martial arts before attending Taijiquan classes taught by one of my teachers, Betsy Chapman. At some point Betsy suggested that he take private lessons with me. We've been working on the Yang style long form, push hands, and martial applications, as well as some weapons and Liu He Ba Fa for a few years. Randy supplements this training with online classes in Chen style, Bagua Palm, and Japanese sword practices.

MARY ANN STANGIL

Mary Ann was studying Chinese martial arts and Qigong in neighboring Lehigh County, PA when she attended a World Tai Chi Day event at Kutztown University. There she saw me demonstrate Liu He Ba Fa and decided that it was something she wanted to learn. Over several years Mary Ann has traveled to take one-on-one lessons with me. She has been teaching Qigong for senior citizens in Lehigh County.

JACK LESNIEWSKI

Jack began taking Taiji lessons with me after retirement from corporate management. Over the years He has studied traditional Yang style, modern simplified variations and short Chen and Sun barehand routines. In addition, we mix in some Liu He Ba Fa and weapons training.

JOSEPH LI

Joe is a Doctor of Neurology with a lifetime of martial arts experience. After attending a few group lessons, he decided to begin private lessons. He has learned the Yang style long barehand form and continues working on push hands and practical applications.

Finding ways to answer student's questions and explain difficult concepts has led me to dig for deeper understanding of these arts. Seeing their progress is a reward for me as well as them. I owe them all my thanks.

Lessons:

Try to answer students' questions.

Teaching can lead to better understanding.

Students can be inspirations.

RECOMMENDED READING

The Tao of Tai-Chi Chuan
  Jou, Tsung Hwa

Taijiquan: The Art of Nurturing, The Science of Power
  Dr. Yang Yang

Taijiquan
  Professor Li Deyin

Practical Tai Chi training
  Jesse Tsou

The Taijiquan Classics (Translations)
  Barbara Davis

Foundations of Traditional Taijiquan
  Sam Masich

Qigong Empowerment
  Shou-Yu Liang

Any Taiji or Qigong books by:
  Dr. Yang Jwing-Ming

ABOUT THE AUTHOR

Jan Gyomber PhD is a long-time practitioner of martial and energy arts. He has studied with dozens of experts in these fields. A certified advanced instructor, Mr. Gyomber has taught hundreds of students Taijiquan (Tai Chi) and Qigong over the course of more than three decades. He has been awarded gold medals at USWU and ICMAC national championships, and at the age of 69 was named Men's age 46 and over Tai Chi Grand Champion of the 2022 International Chinese Martial Arts Championship while collecting five gold medals in barehand and weapons divisions.

Mr. Gyomber has served on the board of directors of the National Qigong Association and on their instructor certification committee. He has presented workshops at NQA national conferences and for the Taijiquan Enthusiasts Organization festivals, also acting as emcee at some of these gatherings.

During the 2009 International Tai Chi Chuan Symposium in Nashville, Tennessee, Jan served as venue manager/host for presentations by the Grandmasters of the five main styles of Taiji.

In 2015 the United Fellowship of Martial Artists inducted Jan into their Hall of Fame. He has also been inducted into the Berks County (PA) Rock and Roll Hall of Fame for drums, guitar, and sound reinforcement.

At the time of this writing, he continues to live and teach in Berks County, Pennsylvania.

TEACHERS AND LESSONS

Ann Hechler (Yoga)
Relaxation with proper body alignment leading to flexibility
Breath control
Awareness of Prana or life energy
Patience
Value of meditation
How to teach

Jerry Boyer (Karate)
Show respect for the teacher
Self-defense techniques

Byron Mellinger (Aikido)
Cooperation
Sensitivity to the energy of others
Use of "internal" energy to support movement
Awareness of one's center

Rick Marth (Taiji)
Standing post training
Relaxation
Alignment
Repetition

Flexibility in Teaching Method
Dantian awareness
Reliance on the Taiji Classics

Marie Perfect (Tuning forks and Gems)
Use of mineral and acoustic modalities to affect body energetics
Improved energetic sensitivity

Carolyn Jaffe and Judy Mellor (Energy healing)
Introduction to energy healing

Betsy Chapman and Sara Gellhorn (Taiji)
Reinforcement of Taiji and Qigong basic principles and theory
Addition of agility, sensitivity, and fajin training
Use of multiple teaching approaches
Expansion of horizons
Situational etiquette
Awareness of the larger Taiji family

Jose Johnson (Taiji)
Dress well to perform
Incorporate silk reeling into your Taiji practice
Be friendly and willing to share any expertise

Nick and Kathy Gracenin (Taiji and Energetics)
Proper use of the eyes in Taiji
Use of hips to change direction with fluidity and stability
Weapon training to improve energy expansion
Martial applications of Taiji movements
Pay attention to energetic and postural alignment

Peter Warr (Taiji)
Challenge yourself to work a little harder to progress, especially
while young

Practice applications carefully – don't injure your training partners
Investigate usage – don't be misled by the names of the movements
Challenge and give encouragement to your students

Nick Scrima (Taiji)
All Taiji movements have martial applications
Strive to find the correct meaning and use of movements
Friendship through martial arts

Dorian Able (Yoga and Reiki)
Yoga is good supplemental training for Taiji.
Reiki training can improve sensitivity to one's own and other's energy.
Reiki training can improve one's ability to affect energy movement in their own and other's bodies.

Pat Rice (Organizer)
Taiji practitioners are all part of a large family.
Be willing to learn from other teachers and styles to enrich your knowledge and enjoyment.

Shou-Yu Liang (Martial arts and Qigong)
A small gift can help make a personal connection.
Importance of a strong foundation
Understanding the difference between self-defense and martial art
Study the basics well, then make the art your own
Reverse breathing
Importance of meditation
Differentiate between martial and health Qigong
Balance belief with skepticism
Research before adopting a strange new practice
Qi = energy + information + essence

Felix Chang (Qigong)
Qigong breath and meditation methods
"Conquer yourself!"

Daniel Lee (Taiji)
Be friendly and respectful when working with others.
Taiji ideas can be applied to other arts.

Sam Masich (Taiji)
Postural alignment
Relaxation
Mental pondering
Humor
Friendship
Document information for future practitioners.

Yang Zhenduo (Taiji)
Functional structure
Relaxed, natural breath
Energy expands out from the center.
Hard work produces results.

Yang Jun (Taiji)
Turn your head to the direction you are looking.
Keep some pressure on front foot during empty stances.
Yang Taijiquan has still, slow, and fast practices.

Yang Jwing-Ming (Taiji and Qigong)
Dedicated research and practice can lead to achievement.
Appreciate and acknowledge those who helped you.
Use modern science to test ancient traditions.
Ponder and test teachings, don't accept blindly.
Goal of practice is to become a better person.
Pass on what you have learned.

Wei Lun Huang (Taiji)
After slowly learning Taijiquan movements well, learn to do them quickly.
Feel opponents' connection to the ground by trying to sense their feet.

Holly Sweeney (Taiji)
Learn to effectively use your shoulder blades and surrounding muscles.
Let pain of injuries help to teach you proper form.

Li Deyin (Taiji)
Clearly show the differences between correct and incorrect movements.
Work hard but have fun.

Yang Yang (Taiji)
Keep awareness and energy in both arms.
Do not enter the fight.

Yang Ying (Music and Qigong)
Music and sound are effective healing modalities.
Be open and friendly.

National Qigong Association
Running a large organization can be both difficult and worthwhile.
Developing organizational skills is important to a professional teacher.
There is value to sharing knowledge and belonging to a community.

Zhongxian Wu (Qigong)
Practicing basics deeply is advanced training.

2009 International Tai Chi Symposium
Taiji, regardless of style is all one family.
Large events take a lot planning, adaptability, and effort, but can
be worth it.

Helen Wu (Taiji)
Be kind, it will be noticed and appreciated.

Taijiquan Enthusiasts Organization
Connect with a wider community.
Take opportunities to learn from different experts.

Julian Chu (Taiji)
Sink the Qi practice method.
Offer students encouragement.

Steve Higgins (Taiji)
Make Taiji friends. They probably have something valuable to
share.
Practice curved stepping.

Helen Liang (Qigong and Martial Arts)
Qigong and Taiji can have important health benefits.
Don't give up. Recovery from dire circumstances is possible.

Chenhan Yang (Taiji and Liu He Ba Fa)
Both broad and deep knowledge of a subject are helpful when
teaching.

John Lee (Swords and martial culture)
Patience and persistence may be rewarded.
Casual conversation with experts may reveal useful information.
Try to learn about Chinese culture and symbolism.

Pete Voll (Taiji)
Be willing to learn from your peers.
Health problems are not a reason to avoid exercise, but a reason
to do appropriate exercises.

Zhu Tiancai (Taiji)
Be willing to interact with less experienced players to help them
improve.
Be ready to interact with more experienced players so you may
learn.